A Minor Adjustment

A Minor Adjustment

ANDY MERRIMAN

PAN BOOKS

First published 1999 by Pan Books
an imprint of Macmillan Publishers Ltd
25 Eccleston Place, London SW1W 9NF
and Basingstoke

Associated companies throughout the world

ISBN 0 330 36748 X

The author and publishers wish to thank the following who have kindly given permission for use of
copyright materials:
The extracts from 'Lullaby' by W. H. Auden and *A Day in the Death of Joe Egg* by Peter Nichols are
reproduced by permission of Faber and Faber.
'Over The Rainbow' words by E. Y. Harburg. Copyright 1938 E.M.I. catalogue partnership/E.M.I.
Feist Catalog Inc. USA. World-wide print rights controlled by Warner Brothers Publications Inc.
USA/I.M.P. Ltd.
The extract from *The Idyll of Miss Sarah Brown* by Damon Runyon is reproduced by
permission of Constable Publishers.
I am also grateful to the Kingsley family for allowing me to use the quotes from *Count Us In* by Jason
Kingsley and Mitchell Levitz.

Typeset by SetSystems Ltd, Saffron Walden, Essex
Printed and bound in Great Britain by
Mackays of Chatham plc, Chatham, Kent

Lay your sleeping head, my love,
Human on my faithless arm;
Time and fevers burn away
Individual beauty from
Thoughtful children, and the grave
Proves the child ephemeral:
But in my arms till break of day
Let the living creature lie,
Mortal, guilty, but to me
The entirely beautiful.

(From 'Lullaby' by W. H. Auden)

Contents

Contents

Preface

When I was first approached by Susan Hill at Macmillan to write this book about Sarah, I was somewhat daunted by the enormity of the task. Not only was it going to be a lot of work, but more importantly, the book would inevitably involve much breast beating and soul baring. Friends and close family were, I think, a little disquieted about the personal nature of the work, but still very encouraging and my wife, Alison, was thrilled at the prospect, but was also naturally apprehensive. The only person amongst my immediate circle who was absolutely certain about this project was Sarah herself. But then that's Sarah. 100 per cent enthusiastic.

Eighteen months later and Sarah remains delighted. When she asks me what I am doing 'tomorrow' (as in the musical *Annie*, one of Sarah's great favourites, 'tomorrow' holds great importance), and I reply that I am working at home on the computer, she continues, 'Writing about me?' When I nod, she says with great ebullience, 'Oh good, Daddy!'

Although I have addressed areas that are common to all families who have a connection with Down's syndrome, this book is primarily about Sarah and how she fits into our story thus far. We feel that, up until now anyway, this is 'a success story'. I don't, however, mean to suggest that she is a representative of all children with Down's syndrome because children with Down's syndrome are all individuals with their own characters and idiosyncrasies.

I am also aware that many parents reading this will have children who suffer from serious health problems or are just physically unable to do very much. There are parents who are still striving for the basic educational rights and those whose children will never be able to achieve any kind of independence – even if given the opportunity.

I have read heart-rending letters in the Down's Syndrome Association newsletter from parents of children who for whatever reason are making very little progress and are understandably irritated by families like ours who can boast of their child's achievements. It is easy to become self-satisfied when I think of Sarah and how much she has done, but we must not forget that for some people having a child with disabilities can be an ordeal and no amount of support, opportunities or resources will ever be enough.

Although I have learned much about Down's syndrome in the last five years, the more I researched the book the more I realized what a huge subject this really is. I am also aware that there are large areas that I have not dealt with in the detail they deserve and some that I have not covered at all. I have not discussed the issue of cultural differences, as I believe there is probably a whole book to be written on this subject and to try to incorporate it in a few pages would be unfair.

Whilst I do think terminology is extremely important, you will see that throughout the book I refer to Down's syndrome and not Down syndrome, which seems to be the trendier expression at the moment and is used widely in the United States and in some places in the United Kingdom. Current thinking seems to be that the man who identified the syndrome and gave it its name, Dr Langdon Down, didn't have Down's syndrome and therefore it should be referred to as Down syndrome. I'm afraid I don't quite understand this as we refer to other medical conditions such as 'Turret's syndrome' and not 'Turret syndrome', 'Huntington's chorea' not 'Huntington chorea' and no one is suggesting Einstein suffered from 'Relativity' by calling it 'Einstein's Relativity'.

I have never had so much assistance and support in any writing project that I have been involved with previously, but then three-minute sketches and situation comedies don't elicit this sort of profound analysis. Thanks, firstly, to my editor, Susan Hill, whose initial interest and positive feeling for this project made it happen. She has continued to guide me skilfully and her quiet confidence has been inestimable.

I am extraordinarily grateful to my 'unofficial researcher', Susannah Seyman, information officer at the Down's Syndrome Association, for her vast knowledge, tireless enthusiasm and incredible efficiency and Maureen Murdock for reading the manuscript so enthusiastically and for her insightful and invaluable comments. Thanks also to Gillian Bird and Sue Buckley at Down Syndrome Educational Trust and family members for their support and contributions – especially my dad, Eric Merriman, for reading each new chapter with great interest and constructive analysis.

Our friends have provided extraordinary support from the day Sarah was born and a mention must be made of Sarah's special godparents, Annie Souter, who has helped me overcome my Luddite tendencies at the computer, and Paul Kelly, who first suggested writing the radio show about Sarah.

I would like to thank the people who have helped Sarah to develop into the person she is: the staff at PALACE, the Norwood Family Centre, the Sabbagh family and Hilary Stumpf, Ruth Meyers and Jackie Gibb at Hilltop playgroup, and all the staff at Bounds Green school – especially Sarah Stubbs, Anita Brady, Bonnie Erdwin-John, Lucy Rodgers and Kim Brough. I cannot name all the health professionals who have helped Sarah over the years, but I would like a special mention for Heather Mackinnon, Gilly Kennedy, Carol Phillips, Susie Gaffin, Sarah Loxton, Heather Cadd and Marie Watson.

Thanks also to our mentors in Los Angeles, the Hixon family, and Emily Perl Kingsley for permission to reprint 'Welcome to

Holland' and I'm sure a lot of parents will also be grateful to her for helping to bring *Sesame Street* to our screens.

I would also like to mention the staff at Alexandra Park Library, the 'Hi-low' poker school, Paul Purnell, Stephen Edwards for his sound advice, my colleagues at the Whittington Hospital, especially Heulwen Morgan, Alice O'Neill and Sebastian Kraemer, for their contributions. I am greatly indebted to all the fathers of children with Down's syndrome for their time and contributions to Paterfamilias Territory and I also wish to acknowledge that I have borrowed shamelessly from the research of Brian Stratford, Cliff Cunningham, Sarah Boston and Michael Bérubé. Thank you.

I am also grateful to the BBC for being able to include scenes from the radio show *Minor Adjustment* and would like to thank everyone connected with the series.

Finally, I must make a special mention of Allie for her great support, dedication and encouragement. Apart from being my sternest full-time critic, she was also my part-time co-author. Without her, this labour of love would not have been created.

A.M.

Foreword

It has always surprised me that a majority of people really believe that 'things ain't what they used to be'. Of course the 'good old days' were halcyon crime free days and we had a drug and violence free society that we are all the worse for losing. Interestingly, while we are told we are losing our values – family, spiritual and moral – we have also been losing many of the prejudices and stigmas that have haunted us for centuries.

Of course, a person's view may only be judged in the context of the age in which he lives. What seems unenlightened now, may well sound at best naive in a few years' time.

Forty-five years ago, doctors told my uncle and my aunt, who had just given birth to a baby with Down's syndrome, that there was nothing to be done but feed and clothe her and keep her happy. No education would produce any useful results and she would, in effect, prove to be a burden to them until the day she died, probably by the time she was twenty. Well I suppose in a way she was a burden to them, although most of the time a joyful and loveable burden and never one they wanted to rid themselves of. But oh, if she had been born forty years later!

Nowadays there are approximately two babies with Down's syndrome born each day in Britain. It is of course a terrible shock to parents expecting and wanting a picture perfect baby, but each day the potential of these children to live a fulfilled and self-sufficient life increases. They have a head start on most of us. They are naturally friendly and caring, and if they have problems as time goes on, as my cousin Linda certainly did, the root usually lies in the early years of frustrated potential.

Linda died five years ago at the age of forty. A major escape for her, as for many of us, was the TV, and over the years she became my biggest fan. Because of Linda I got involved with the Down's Syndrome Association, becoming a patron, and presenting the annual achievement awards. The achievements are in context: older winners perhaps sustaining a steady job and living in the community, and the younger ones tending to have gold medals and world championships in anything from riding bicycles up mountains to art and photography, not to mention acting. At the awards lunch the actor, Timmy Lang, performed by last ever *Dr Who* episode in its entirety, playing all the parts, and performing mine a lot better than I ever did.

With this behind me it was a surprising coincidence to be asked by Andy and Eric to play the father in their situation comedy for radio, *Minor Adjustment*. The 'situation', you see, is a family with a child who has Down's syndrome, based on Andy's own family and his daughter, Sarah.

I defy anyone to meet Sarah and not fall in love. She is now six years old and as charismatic as anyone I have met. She was often in the studio with us, adding bits and pieces to the script, as well as undertaking some deft editing in the best traditions of the star! I think it was a major step forward to write the radio series and get it on the air not least because what seems an extraordinary idea for comedy is so natural and funny when you hear it.

Not content to sit on his laurels, Andy has gone one step further.

I'm sure you'll enjoy this book. It captures Sarah's spirit and is both encouraging to those who have a child with Down's syndrome and enlightening to those who haven't.

Peter Davison

1. Expecting the Unexpected

'Stand by studio. Quiet please. Right, let's go for a take. The tape's running.'

We are in Studio 6A at BBC Broadcasting House in central London. In front of the control room, there is a large area which is sparsely furnished with screens, a table and in the middle a couple of free-standing, heavy, wooden doors, leading nowhere. There is a circle of hard, plastic chairs remaining in position from the earlier read-through of the script and a trolley bearing the debris of our coffee break: styrofoam cups, synthetic stirrers, and half used packets of sugar alongside the few remaining biscuits and an empty miniature carton of apple juice. The studio is littered with props. There are bottles to be opened, glasses to be clinked, newspapers and letters to be rustled and money to be jingled. All adding to the authentic background sounds and atmosphere of the family portrayed in this, our latest radio series.

The producer bends down to speak to the pretty, fair-haired little girl – rather small for her four years, who is featured in this scene. 'Now, you've been playing in the park and you come through this front door with Peter. You run up to Sam and then you say the line that you have learned. All right?' She nods professionally. The producer returns to the glass-panelled control room, cues the studio manager and the action begins.

Sarah follows her directions perfectly, running, somewhat ungainly, from one side of the room to the other and bursts through 'the front door'.

'Mummy ... Mummy,' she shouts gleefully as she throws herself into her pretend mother's arms.

'Swing, slide, seesaw.'

'Yes, darling, I know you've been to the park. And good girl, that's nearly a whole sentence – well done!'

The toddler, obviously delighted with this praise, hugs her mother voraciously and kisses her on the cheek. 'Lunch now?'

'Mummy' laughs. 'That's not in the script, Sarah, but the rest was jolly good.'

The producer's disembodied voice booms across the studio floor from behind the glass panel. 'No, but that entrance was excellent. Still, I'd like to try it again if we may, the door opening was a bit loud. We'd better just check the mikes.' The green light goes off and the studio manager leaves her seat to examine the position of the microphones.

As one of the writers of the show, I was sitting next to Gareth Edwards, the producer. I couldn't have been more proud of Sarah, who was not only one of the stars of the show, but also my daughter. She had performed and behaved beautifully, the cast members had been extremely patient and kind to her and her presence added an authenticity to the family drama.

'No, this wasn't how the script was supposed to read' seemed an adroit, if inadvertent description of Sarah's life thus far.

It shouldn't have been in the script that our daughter would be born with Down's syndrome, that we might never come to terms with having a disabled child and that if we couldn't cope we might just have to give her away. Her four-year existence had already provided us with enough worries, questions and emotional turbulence to last a lifetime. But we also never dreamed that she would be featured in a comedy-drama, written by myself and her grandfather.

Naturally, Sarah's first appearance on BBC Radio 4 couldn't have been more different than her original debut at the Whittington Hospital's labour ward on 9 January 1992, when we certainly did not feel that 'a star was born'.

There had been no reason to believe that the birth of our

second child was going to be much different from that of our first two years earlier. Although he was nearly two weeks late and the labour was long and tortuous, Daniel's arrival had been fairly straightforward. Well, it was certainly straightforward for me – I just watched. It was slightly more arduous for my wife, Alison, although I have to say she went through the whole process without even an aspirin.

Being of the liberal persuasion and also living in North London, it was apparently mandatory that we attend the local Natural Childbirth Trust group and so we did have some idea of what was supposed to happen. Fortunately our particular group had been informative without being precious – there wasn't a beanbag in sight and none of the men felt envious or guilty about not being able to breastfeed. Of course I did have to explain to Allie that 'natural childbirth' didn't mean giving birth without wearing make-up.

Daniel had been born at the Whittington Hospital where both Allie and I had worked as social workers and when Allie became pregnant with Sarah, she remained under the care of the same consultant obstetrician. There weren't any problems during the pregnancy and apart from the usual scans which all appeared to be normal, Allie also had the Alfa Feta Protein blood test which gives an approximate idea of any possible birth defects. The results did not show anything unusual.

The night before Sarah was born, we were watching a Paul Simon concert on television and he sang a song called 'Born at the Wrong Time'. Allie had already started to go into labour and we both remarked that as it was likely that the baby would now be born in the middle of the night, these words seemed some-what prophetic. Although I was being flippant, Allie later said that this song had surprisingly filled her with panic and a sense of foreboding.

As Allie's contractions grew stronger, I rang my mother who had arranged to come and stay and look after Daniel. As soon as she arrived, we sped to the hospital, which was only about fifteen minutes away. After an initial examination, the process seemed to slow down and at about two o'clock in the morning, it was decided that I could go home, but Allie should remain in hospital. I rang back the next morning and Allie said that there was no change in her condition and she was no further forward. Half an hour later she called to say that things were now moving and I'd better get there quickly.

Of course, we now live in an enlightened age where fathers are expected to be at the birth of their offspring. No self-respecting dad would want to miss out on this extraordinary occasion – an experience that will remain with him for the rest of his life. A momentous, spiritually uplifting and mystical event with which no other feeling can compare. The togetherness of sharing an unparalleled joy with your lifelong partner. But then there *is* that faint hope that maybe . . . well . . . maybe . . . your mad dash to the hospital might just be too late and oh my God – how tragic – you've missed the whole thing. The baby has been born, bathed and is looking almost human, the screaming and rending of clothes is over, the blood and unspeakable gore has been cleared up and you are left to utter a calm, 'Well done' in hushed tones. Your loved one is asleep and you are left in peace to light up your cigar and smoke reflectively on what you have thankfully just missed.

Not this time . . . When I reached the labour ward at about nine o'clock, Allie was having regular and painful contractions and although the moment of delivery was obviously imminent, I would be present and politically correct at the birth.

At 9.45 a.m. our baby arrived as if propelled from a huge gun – a human cannonball who seemed to fly through the air into the safe arms of one of the two midwives who were in attendance. It was a girl – just as we had wanted – our luck had held out again. We now had a boy and a girl. 'It's my dream come true,' Allie remarked. It was about to turn into a nightmare.

Sarah was quite blue and seemed to be struggling for air and my first remark to Allie was 'She looks like a little Buddha.' Sarah was put into an incubator and very soon her colour became a more healthy looking pink. I went off to telephone both sets of grandparents and inform them that all was well and that their first granddaughter had arrived safe and sound.

Whilst I was away, Allie was naturally engrossed with her newborn child and studied every detail. She seemed perfect in every way and even her expression portrayed a curiously independent air. But the longer this loving examination continued, Allie started to feel that something was wrong. She looked more carefully at Sarah's face and noticed a number of particular features that she had seen in some other children. Sarah had small, protruding ears, a round face and a wide bridge of the nose.

A foreboding image began to appear in her mind and desperately trying to remember other characteristics, she checked for more signs.

There was a large gap between Sarah's big toe and the rest of her toes, and her fingers were short and stubby. She grabbed Sarah's hand and searched for the palmic crease, but couldn't see a significant line. Sarah's weight had been above average and she was already starting to breastfeed. Perhaps, in the aftermath of giving birth and the resulting unreality, her imagination had taken over? Confused and her mind in a whirl, Allie told the midwife that she thought that Sarah had Down's syndrome features, hoping to be reassured with something like, 'Oh, all babies look a bit funny and squashed when they're born.' Frighteningly, the midwife replied by saying, 'I'd better call the paediatrician.'

I returned ten minutes later and on entering the delivery room, Allie told me what had happened. I looked to the midwife for some instant reassurance, but she was busying herself with cleaning up and was clearly too engrossed to confirm or deny.

During the birth, Allie had been torn and was now being stitched. She seemed not to notice the pain and could only stare at Sarah, hoping that all was well. I took Sarah out of her cot, held her in my arms and stared at her. It was immediately apparent that she did indeed have Down's syndrome. How could I not have noticed the obvious features when she was first born? Her eyes were almond shaped, her neck was short and thick and the back of her head seemed somewhat flat.

'What do you think?' asked Allie.

'I don't know,' I said. 'It's too difficult to tell.'

'She's very floppy, isn't she?'

'So would you be if you'd just been born,' I said weakly.

We both knew the reality, but felt too helpless to confront the truth and I felt that I had to be comforting and optimistic whilst Allie was still receiving medical attention.

After what seemed like an eternity, but was actually only about fifteen minutes, the consultant paediatrician arrived with a junior doctor. We both knew Dr Mackinnon well as we had worked with her. Both doctors examined Sarah whilst I sat on the bed holding Allie's hand.

Dr Mackinnon finished her examination, turned and walked towards us. She was nodding as she approached and said that, yes, she did think that Sarah had Down's syndrome. She apologized as if she bore some fault or blame and hugged us both. She said that the diagnosis would have to be confirmed by a blood test and we should have the results within a week. There was just a very slight chance that the diagnosis would not be established, but we all knew that there would be no reprieve. Dr Mackinnon offered us some kind words and said she thought we should be left alone to talk, but that she would come back later. She, her colleague and the midwives left us on our own. I picked Sarah up, held her closely in my arms and whispered to her, 'Oh Sarah . . . Sarah . . . what have you done? You've got it all wrong . . .'

We both cried and my thoughts turned to the adults with

Down's syndrome that I had worked with as a social worker nearly twenty years before. The image that had always stuck in my mind was that of middle-aged women, with hair in ribbons and attired like little girls in ill-fitting dresses, drab cardigans and white, knee-high socks. These sorts of people were supposed to be clients of mine – people that I was employed to help – not my daughter, who was supposed to be bright and beautiful. These people attended adult training centres for 'the handicapped' performing menial tasks for little pleasure or reward. My daughter was going to go to university and become a doctor or a barrister. People with Down's syndrome were patronized, joked about and exploited and still referred to as 'mongols'.

This wasn't how it was supposed to be.

I went to phone the grandparents – only this time to tell them that the news wasn't so good. Allie's parents had gone out so I spoke to her sister. She could barely believe what I told her. She said she would talk to her parents and I was somewhat grateful that I wouldn't have to undertake this task. I rang my parents again and this time talked to my mother. She is an extremely stoical person and she took the news calmly, barely commenting. I was relieved about this because I really felt too distressed to discuss it. She said that she would tell my dad for which I was equally grateful.

I returned to the labour ward, where two close women friends, Pat Dimitrovic and Annie Souter who also worked in the hospital with us, had arrived to see Allie. They looked pale and shocked and we all embraced. I started to cry as soon as I saw them and none of us knew quite what to say. Although Allie is Jewish and we are not religious, we have chosen godparents for the children – not in a spiritual sense, but in the hope that they can enjoy a special relationship with an adult outside the family. We had asked Annie to be Sarah's godmother and the only thing that I could think to ask was whether the fact that Sarah had Down's syndrome would make any difference and whether she would still wish to be godmother. Naturally, Annie said that of course she would still wish to take on this responsibility and that the situation would make her even more determined to be closely involved in Sarah's life. It was strange how this unexpected turn of events – even at this early stage – made us question everything. Soon after, Allie and I even discussed whether we should still call the baby Sarah, as she was now going to be patently different from how we had first pictured our new daughter.

After Pat and Annie had left, we talked to one of the midwives, who had delivered Sarah. It transpired that she had a thirty-year-old brother who had Down's syndrome. She told us that he was studying accountancy and had a girlfriend and was leading a pretty full life. She was the first person of many, who in years to come would give us encouraging examples of friends or relatives with Down's syndrome.

Although we were still in a state of shock, it was important to hear something so positive. Even at that time I thought how much of a coincidence it was that from the moment of birth, Sarah had a link with another person who had Down's syndrome.

When we were left on our own once again, we tried to make some sense of it all. 'We are going to keep her, aren't we?' Allie asked. Without thinking, I replied, 'Of course we are.' I seriously hadn't considered any other option at this stage, but it transpired that Allie was thinking of clients of hers who had not kept their baby with Down's syndrome. The husband had refused to accept the baby's condition and the wife had been put in the impossible position of choosing between her husband and her child. She chose the husband.

Even a couple of hours after Sarah's birth, we were both quite clear that we wanted to take her home. There didn't seem to be any other realistic alternative for us, but it was actually very helpful when the consultant obstetrician, Miss Morgan, came to see us later. She felt that as social workers and supposedly responsible people, who had counselled people in our very position, we would feel that we had to cope and that there would be an assumption that we would just get on with it. She made it clear that if Sarah's arrival was too much to bear and that we felt under too much pressure to manage, we should consider having her fostered to give us time to think about the future. Although, from our work, we both knew that this was an option, it was very important that it was spelled out to us so clearly.

We did have an obligation to Sarah, but we also had a responsibility to Daniel and to each other. Sarah was now part of our family, but not at any cost.

Later that morning, Allie and Sarah were transferred to a post-natal ward. Fortunately they were allocated a room to themselves so that at least we would have some privacy. By this time, I had really had enough. I actually couldn't wait to get away from the hospital and even from Allie as I no longer knew what to say to her. The strain of being the main source of support was beginning to affect me and my words of reassurance now sounded hollow. It had been agreed that I would collect Daniel from his childminder and bring him back to the hospital to meet his new sibling as soon as possible and this was my chance to escape!

We had all got very excited at the prospect of Daniel's reaction. Now, this trip seemed horribly daunting and I couldn't bear the thought of seeing him. Although he was only two years and three months and obviously wouldn't understand all the implications of Sarah's birth, he would soon be able to gauge my mood.

Thankfully, Annie took charge and insisted on driving me. When Daniel was born, I couldn't wait to go into the nearest toyshop and celebrate by buying him the inevitable teddy bear. This time it was different. I felt numb and distressed and I certainly didn't feel like bounding into a shop and excitedly choosing something for Sarah. It certainly didn't seem like a time to celebrate and although I felt that I was already letting Sarah down, I just couldn't face buying her anything. On the way to collect Daniel, Annie bought a wonderful teddy bear for Sarah.

Prior to us leaving the hospital, Annie had telephoned the childminder – also called Annie – to tell her what had happened and so by the time we arrived at her house, she was already aware of events. Being an ex-nursing sister at Great Ormond Street Hospital for Children, she was quite used to drama and crises and was extremely sympathetic and calm. I went into the room where Daniel was playing and broke down in tears as soon as I saw him. This wasn't the sister that he was supposed to have and would he now be responsible for her for the rest of his life? I told him that he had a baby sister and although he had said he wanted a brother, he seemed happy enough. Amazingly he didn't seem to notice my anguish, but I was already wondering how and when we would tell him about Sarah – he was obviously too young to understand now, but how soon would he realize that something was wrong?

Annie drove Daniel and me back to the hospital by which time my mother and Allie's parents were there. No one quite knew what to say, but everybody was trying to make it as 'normal' as possible, whilst acknowledging the reality of the situation. Not long after, one of the nurses popped in and said that Sarah was due to have a scan in another department. I quickly volunteered to take her as I was finding it very difficult to face the family without breaking down.

As it is common in children with Down's syndrome to have heart defects, we had been warned, soon after Sarah's birth, that she would have to have a scan. I was advised to take Sarah to the Special Care Baby Unit, where another consultant paediatrician was waiting for us. I thus found myself pushing a large, transparent hospital cot, containing my tiny daughter, around the very same corridors where I had worked for nearly ten years. How often had I casually directed relatives or patients to an appointment, where the outcome might change their whole lives?

I had worked briefly as the paediatric social worker and had probably discussed with parents the need for a scan such as this. Now, the situation was somewhat different.

Inevitably, on the way, I met quite a few colleagues and acquaintances – all of whom were interested in my new daughter, but all of whom I wanted to keep at a distance and not to have to explain what had happened and what I was doing. We finally reached the Unit and walked past the half dozen incubators containing babies of minute size – one or two as small as my hand. We were shown into the side room where Sarah was to be scanned and I was introduced to Dr Broadhurst, whom I also knew. We chatted politely for a few minutes until Sarah was connected to the various electrodes, leads and paraphernalia that would determine her future.

As the various clouds and fuzzy images appeared on the screen, I looked down at this tiny creature and felt very little for her other than sympathy that she had to start her life in such disastrous circumstances.

Perhaps, if she did have an inoperable heart condition, it might be so serious that she might not survive for very long. Perhaps if it was serious, she might have to undergo major surgery on a number of occasions. Perhaps, if she was not going to have any quality of life and with a future of poor health and a severe learning disability, then perhaps, it might be better for everyone – especially her – if she just passed away . . .

I was looking at my daughter – not even a day old – and wishing her dead.

Although *A Minor Adjustment* is written in my name, Allie has, of course, contributed substantially to the book and helped me a great deal. It was important for both of us that she was also able to put some of her thoughts and feelings into words. The following is the first of several chapters by her.

2. *Memories and Reflections,*
9/10 January 1992

The hospital porter came to wheel Sarah and me to the post-natal ward. I wondered if he considered why I looked so glum after what is meant to have been such a glorious event. After all, there was this sweet, newborn baby, sleeping calmly beside me.

I knew my parents would be coming soon and two thoughts struck me about how each would react. How on earth would my mother take the news? She had helped me take such tremendous care with every part of my pregnancy: ante-natal exercises (she used to be a physiotherapist), insisting on healthy eating and generally preventing me from doing too much whenever she could. Where had my mother's vigilance got us?

More superficial, perhaps, was the thought about my father. Would he bring his videocamera and record the early hours in hospital, as he had done with his other grandchildren?

I was wheeled into the side room of the post-natal ward and tried to avoid the looks of the other mothers who were milling around. I felt that I was in another world. The midwife helped me into bed and she left. I was alone with Sarah for the first time.

I looked at her, peacefully sleeping, and felt nothing. No rush of love, of protectiveness or even pity. I picked her up mechanically and held her to try to evoke some emotion. I felt dead and returned Sarah to her cot.

My mother and father appeared and, soon after, Andy's mother (his dad was unwell and couldn't visit). Despite their obviously strained expressions, they were all loving and caring and I began to talk about Sarah having Down's syndrome. They listened, without letting me know how they felt, preferring to let me talk. I, in turn, wasn't ready to hear their reactions.

My father had indeed brought his videocamera and filmed the scene from time to time – at least this was no different from Daniel's birth. I loved him for this as I did my mother for not even hinting at her own anxiety and pain.

Two young boys burst through the door – my nephews, Tom and Nicholas – to view their new baby cousin and then my sister, Carey, appeared. I felt so envious of her; she had two 'normal' children and was never going to have to face the lifetime of hardship that I was sure was ahead of us. Carey was warm and welcoming of Sarah whilst giving me space to make sense of what was happening.

What I only appreciated much later was how suddenly Sarah had changed everything for every family member. My parents were now grandparents of a Down's syndrome baby. Carey was an aunt of a Down's syndrome baby and Tom and Nicholas were cousins of a Down's syndrome baby. New identities for everyone. The ripples were to go on and on.

Later, Andy returned with Daniel, who was wearing, I remember, his yellow Mickey Mouse sweatshirt. 'What have I done to you?' I whispered to myself as he came running in to see his new sister. I had planned not to be holding my second baby when Daniel visited as all the books said this could help to reduce the levels of jealousy in the older sibling. That was one problem I didn't have. I wasn't holding her because I didn't feel like holding her. Photos were taken and we posed rigidly. For Daniel's sake I tried to look happy, but inside I was full of dread. Eventually the family departed and Sarah and I were left to our own devices.

On the door of my side room was a sign which read: 'Do not disturb. Speak to a midwife before entering.' I was glad about this as I was longing for some privacy and felt that I wanted to cocoon myself away for ever. However, this sign seemed to act – not as a caveat – as an open invitation to all and sundry to drop in. I can honestly say that for the next couple of days my room was like Piccadilly Circus in the height of the tourist season!

The news of Sarah's birth spread like wildfire through the hospital and well-meaning staff members from a multitude of disciplines all felt that they were ideally placed to pay me an unofficial visit. The hospital chaplain, the ante-natal sister, labour ward midwives, health advocates, interpreters, various consultants, an obstetric physiotherapist and a number of social work colleagues as well as close friends and friends of friends all popped in.

This furious activity served the function of keeping reality at bay. In retrospect, it seemed the more I talked to people, the more I could keep my mantle of control. I think what I was terrified of more than anything was the feeling of being pitied or of Sarah being pitied. I was going to lead by example; I heard myself saying brave things about our lives becoming enriched, about the challenge ahead and about how I felt our family would become closer than ever.

When we were finally left alone again, I realized I was in overdrive, almost in a state of elation and I certainly could not begin to sleep. Sarah was very undemanding. She fed well at my breast and dropped off to sleep. If only I could follow her lead. I was more drained and exhausted than I had ever been in my life, but sleep was to evade me for the whole period I spent in hospital and for much of the next month.

Soon after midnight, there was a knock at the door. It was the junior doctor, who had been present in the labour ward when Sarah had first been examined. Although it was late, we talked for quite a while and I was extremely impressed by her awareness, sensitivity and philosophical approach to what had happened. It seemed to consolidate some of the frantic machinations of the day's activities. She eventually took blood from Sarah, which would be sent away for likely confirmation of her diagnosis. Sarah screamed as the blood was drawn and I was shocked to realize that I was so emotionally detached that I felt nothing about her cries of pain. I felt ashamed and guilty.

For the rest of the night I was in what seemed to be 'an icy grip' – a phrase I coined for the unwelcome feeling I was to experience intermittently for the next few weeks. I can only think of it as the palpable evidence of panic and the abject fear within me.

I continued my automated routine of feeding and changing Sarah when necessary, hardly wanting to look at the being, who twenty-four hours before had kicked within me. In retrospect, I was lucky that Sarah was able to breastfeed so easily – something that newborn babies with Down's syndrome sometimes have trouble with. If she hadn't, I don't honestly know how I would have been able to cope.

The following morning, a kitchen domestic bearing tea arrived and wished me a cheery good morning. She looked at the baby and asked if it was a boy or a girl. I told her it was a girl and then felt a sudden need to tell her all about Sarah. I would have to face telling people sooner or later – why not now?

'Sarah has Down's syndrome,' I mumbled.

She let this sink in for a moment, looked at me and said, 'What have you been smoking?'

I tried to explain the facts, but there seemed no point as this accusation seemed so hurtful. I felt a complete failure and looked away until she had left the room. She was soon followed by the cleaner, whom I also told about Sarah.

'Oh,' she said. 'You're a social worker here, aren't you?'

'Yes,' I said.

'Well, you've been listening to too many problems – this is what has made this happen.'

I could hardly believe what I was hearing, but realized that this was just the start of how we were now going to have to live our lives. Encountering ignorance, and prejudice – always being on the defensive and having to make explanations and excuses. I made a mental note that when I felt much stronger, I would like to mount a campaign to ensure that all hospital staff and ancillary workers were provided with some basic training and information about such situations. They were, after all, at 'the coal face' and would sometimes have to face people in crisis and turmoil.

The frantic visiting stopped after the second day and I had more time to reflect and I thought of a close friend, currently in a room in an ante-natal ward, exactly two floors down from mine. She was also expecting her second child and I remembered a recent outing with our sons, sharing with each other our secret hopes for a little girl this time.

Since then, there had been some complications in her pregnancy, resulting in her admission to hospital for several weeks. I had made a few visits to her side room, feeling fortunate but somewhat guilty that I wasn't in her position of being trapped and uncertain about the future. What would she be thinking now? I felt closely bonded to her, but sensed that it would be impossible to now pay her a visit. The depth of our joint fear and pain would overwhelm us both.

Soon after I returned home, she told me that her little girl had only lived for four hours. We sobbed together, but were unable to console each other in our grief. At the time, although I naturally felt very sad for her, it seemed that I was worse off; not only had my child 'died' – I was after all grieving for the child that I didn't now have – but I also had a child that I didn't want. A child that needed looking after and caring for and who might remain like a child for the rest of her life.

One of the midwives requested that I have lunch in the day room with some of the other mothers. I had to refuse as I just couldn't face them. My feelings were so totally opposite to theirs of apparent joy. This was the first time I was to experience just how hard it was to be with other mothers and babies and this was actually to last until Sarah was about four years old. Were we their worst nightmare, did we fill them with dread? We would be a talking point: 'There but for the grace of God go I . . .' All the protocol around the arrival of a new baby was called into question. I longed desperately to stick to the game plan that I knew. I became very anxious to leave hospital. I had a vain hope that once Sarah was in our family's familiar environment, she would begin to feel like she belonged, that she was ours and that my frozen heart would begin to melt. Surely, once she was in what was, after all, her own home, her rights would be established.

I felt tortured by my lack of love for this helpless creature who was so intimately mine. I had expunged Sarah's right to be loved purely on the basis of an extra chromosome.

3. That's Going to Make Shopping Difficult

A doctor goes to a patient and says he has some good news and some bad news. Which would the patient like to hear first?

Patient: I think I'll have the good news.
Doctor: You've got twenty-four hours to live.
Patient: My God, if that's the good news, what's the bad news?
Doctor: I should have told you yesterday.

I had always enjoyed these good news/bad news jokes and I could quote many more should the occasion arise, but now they didn't seem quite so hilarious. It was, ironically, my turn to be the doctor and the patients were my friends and family.

The night after Sarah was born, I went home exhausted and bewildered. Everything had been turned upside-down and it appeared that my life was never going to be the same. I had only spoken to a few people and didn't yet feel like contacting others. There were, of course, a couple of exceptions – friends whom I needed to tell and to talk to and it wouldn't matter what I said or how upset I was.

I had telephoned one of my closest friends, Danny Silverstone, a few hours after Sarah's birth; he was the first friend I rang.

Funnily enough, unlike the family, I didn't dread talking to him, because I knew whatever his reaction would be, it would be truthful and not necessarily protective. The news I was about to impart wasn't tragic – Allie was fine and the baby was alive and kicking – but neither was it exactly blissful.

'Hi Danny, it's Andy.'

'Well, anything to report?' I could hear Danny whispering to his daughter that I was on the phone and in the background I could hear her excitedly asking for news. The feeling of expectation heightened.

'Yes . . . um . . . there is.'

'Well?'

'Well, Allie had a baby girl this morning.'

'Congratulations!' I could hear him telling his daughter that it was a girl. 'That's terrific.'

'Actually, it's not. She's got Down's syndrome.'

There was a long silence and probably for the first time in his life, Danny was lost for words. We spoke briefly – a conversation that Danny has since described as the longest two minutes he has ever spent talking to me – and he then immediately rang Allie on the ward.

When he visited me that evening, there was an air of unreality. I talked about anything that came into my head and wept for the daughter that I had lost and for the new daughter that I had found.

Danny listened to my tearful streams of consciousness and comforted me with honesty and humour – an awareness born from nearly twenty years of friendship. He didn't attempt to tell me how I should be feeling nor did he endeavour to be falsely optimistic. I think that I was in such a state of despair that amazingly no mention was even made of the Spurs win against Norwich in the league cup the previous evening.

In the next couple of days, before Allie came home from hospital, I did start to make contact with friends about the news. Although at the time, it certainly didn't feel that it was helping me to come to terms with the situation, I now realize that it was a very valuable process. I recounted what had happened many times and it seemed that the talking I did in those early days did indeed have a therapeutic effect.

Generally the reactions from people ranged from, 'Jesus Christ, what a nightmare,' to 'So, what's the problem?' and even, 'Sarah will be such a challenge, I'm excited for you both.' I suppose we were grateful for any contact and I would certainly not be critical of anyone's first responses to such dramatic news. I know that in their situation, I just wouldn't have had any idea of what to say or how to say it.

Some years ago, a friend's mother was talking to a neighbour over the back garden fence. She was tearfully explaining that she and her husband hadn't been getting on at all well and there was a possibility that he would leave. The couple didn't really know what was for the best. Should the husband stay for a while in an attempt to make things work or should they opt for a trial separation? He had left temporarily, but had now come back. It was a very difficult and traumatic time for them both. The neighbour sighed heavily, shook her head, threw her hands up in the air in a display of hopelessness and declared, 'That's going to make shopping difficult.'

Whether this was an attempt to say something bland so as not to offend or she just didn't know what to say but felt she had to say something, is difficult to tell. Of course it may be that the neighbour had a genuine concern about possible trolley embarrassment at the supermarket checkout. We shall never know. But I do know that this expression has now worked its way into the family's essential list of idiomatic sayings and is used wherever possible.

Once, in a bed and breakfast establishment in Lochgilphead, Scotland, we came across an elderly man struggling to get down the stairs carrying a dachshund under each arm. 'That's going to make shopping difficult,' I said as I moved out of his way.

But also on hearing news of terrible disasters and personal tragedy this phrase comes to mind, as sometimes the most heartfelt expression of solace or support becomes meaningless. To say, 'How terrible' or 'That's a shame' seems crass. Sometimes it is not possible to put into words how you are feeling and sometimes one doesn't even know what one is feeling.

I am sure that this was true for our family and many of our friends and acquaintances when we told them about Sarah. Mainly they just listened, barely commenting, and certainly not proffering advice at this stage.

We were showered with letters and telephone calls in the weeks after Sarah's birth. We were delighted to hear from people and welcomed this contact with eager anticipation. The volume of correspondence was extraordinary and it was obvious how much care and thought had gone into the messages. It was also evident that the finished article was probably the third or fourth draft and we pictured waste-paper baskets up and down the country overflowing with discarded ambiguous messages of sympathy and congratulations.

Friends whom we hadn't heard from in years contacted us and much of the correspondence commented on the adaptation our lives would have to make and the challenges that lay ahead: 'the unexpected gains to be made' and the awareness of 'the inherently contradictory feelings that you must be experiencing'.

Some mentioned that if Sarah had to be born with Down's syndrome, then she could not have parents better suited to deal with the trials and tribulations that lay ahead. We were flattered, but wondered whether we really were equipped to cope with the future which appeared to be extremely daunting.

A friend from Washington D.C. wrote, '. . . when the external physical circumstances and internal emotions are equally so demanding, you are in some ways your most raw, painfully so; but in other ways there is sometimes the sense that life doesn't get more real or more dear than this, and the senses are heightened to meet that undertaking.' In contrast, one of the most touching communications – from an old school friend – ended in an attempt to resume 'normal service' by asking, 'Could this be Chelsea's year for the FA Cup?'

Of course the reaction that one elicits very much depends on how the news is broken. Here's an example of one way of doing it.

Two elderly sisters who live together decide to go away on holiday. They are, however, worried about leaving their old cat on his own and so ask their next door neighbour to look after him. Unfortunately, three days into their holiday, they receive a letter from the neighbour, stating that the cat has died.

Naturally, the two sisters return home in a distressed state and are also unhappy with the neighbour about how she broke the news so bluntly. 'What you should have done,' says one of the sisters to the hapless neighbour, 'is sent us a postcard saying that the cat is on the roof and is refusing to come down, but not to worry. Then, a few days later, you could have sent us another note saying the cat is down from the roof, but is off his food a little. Then – maybe the following week – you could have written to say that the cat really isn't well and you're a little concerned. Finally, you could have sent us a letter saying that the cat had died.'

The neighbour apologized for being so insensitive and promised to be more thoughtful in the future.

The following summer, the younger of the two sisters decides to have a holiday on her own and entrusts the same neighbour with the care of her older sibling. Whilst on holiday, she receives a postcard from the neighbour which reads, 'Your sister's on the roof and she's refusing to come down . . .'

Whilst not expecting medical staff to follow the above example, it is true that breaking bad news does require sensitivity, tact and the understanding of each particular situation. The importance of how news of the diagnosis is communicated cannot be underestimated. Personal testimony and research show the consequences of this can last a lifetime and there is no doubt that this is crucial in how we cope with the situation.

The Down's Syndrome Association states,

> At best parents are given no information and at worst the
> information that they are given is ill-informed and inaccurate.
> Some parents are still told at the outset that they should not
> expect their child to achieve anything.
>
> It is inevitable that you will feel differently toward your child
> if you are told by a doctor that 'she is unlikely ever to live a
> normal life and is destined for a life of ill-health' than you will if
> you are told that your child is 'different, will need more help
> than most other children and may need some future medical
> care'.

I know of a paediatrician whose nephew has Down's syndrome, and whenever he hears of the birth of a baby with
Down's syndrome in his hospital he rushes to the scene with
photographs of the boy, whom he adores!

This may be somewhat precipitous, but there is no doubt that
these positive feelings will have a lasting effect on the parents'
view of their newborn baby. If parents are treated particularly
insensitively, not only is it likely to affect their view of the child
and the child's future care, but it can also affect the future view
of the medical profession. This is, after all, information that
could alter your whole life.

One continues to hear terrible stories about how the news that
a child has Down's syndrome is broken to the parents. One
mother – within twenty-four hours of the birth of her child –
was advised, 'Watch your daughter carefully. Down's girls are at
high risk for being molested. They are easy prey for paedophiles,'
and another whose obstetrician warned her to expect 'a sickly,
handicapped child who wouldn't have the sense to get out of a
building if it were on fire'. I have heard of a mother who
discovered her baby's diagnosis during a casual chat with a nurse,
who was under the impression that the mother had already been

informed of the situation. Another mother was casually looking at the clipboard at the end of her hospital bed and noticed that on top of one of the pages – in large red letters – were written the words, 'BABY HAS DOWN'S SYNDROME.'

There are a number of parents who have experienced visits by doctors, so shocked and perplexed themselves, that they hurriedly blurt out the facts, do not make eye contact and then beat a hasty retreat. There is, in fact, a debate about whether it should be doctors at all who have the first contact with the parents. Clinicians are the first to admit that communication is not always their strongest suit, they often do not know the parents very well and certainly do not have the time to sit and talk for long periods of time.

We must not forget that doctors have their own frailties and are just as susceptible to emotional pressures. To expect a doctor, who is after all very highly technically skilled, to simultaneously act as an accomplished communicator in what is perhaps the most highly charged and sensitive of situations is indeed asking a great deal. This is not, however, to suggest that the possibility of mastering both areas is not attainable and should not be demanded, but simply to point out that it takes an exceptional individual to excel on both levels. The basis of medicine has to be scientific, but the training of doctors could be broadened to include the skills necessary to meet the overall needs of patients, not just simply the clinical requirements.

We can all remember what we were doing at the time that we heard particularly bad news – the date that Arsenal won the double is etched in my mind for ever and the assassination of President John F. Kennedy is always quoted as an unforgettable moment in our lives. (I've always wondered if Lee Harvey Oswald could remember what he was doing when he heard of Kennedy's death.) In the same way, parents can often remember details such as what they were wearing, the colour of the hospital walls, the atmosphere in the room, the expression on the doctor's face – a sensory snapshot that remains unfaded throughout their lives.

I have been asked to recount the experience on many occasions and it seems to be of great interest to friends and acquaintances exactly how we were told about Sarah. I have told the story so many times that one would think I could almost recall it in a detached, matter of fact manner. Not so. It doesn't matter how many times I recall the event, I am still moved.

Of course, we were in a unique and extremely fortunate situation in that we knew our consultant paediatrician, Heather Mackinnon, very well, and had both worked with her for some years. Allie and I were told in almost 'the ideal' circumstances.

We were together and it was very quickly confirmed that there was a problem. Sarah was present and was continually being held and referred to – thereby conveying her worth. We were in a private place where there was no likelihood of distraction or fear of being overheard. We were given a lot of time and we were in the presence of staff who could later offer us support and counselling. We were given time to be on our own together with our baby after we had been told. We were also advised that we would be able to talk further to Dr Mackinnon the following day. It was important that we had repeated opportunities to discuss what was happening and to try to make sense of it. In retrospect, we were clearly in shock at the time and felt numb and cut off from reality. We needed the medical staff to go over the same information time and time again, as we did not hear or understand every word.

As I have previously mentioned, it was beneficial that the midwife who delivered Sarah was so positive about her own brother who had Down's syndrome. It seems that the early reactions of professionals can reinforce society's rejection of people with disabilities. However, here was someone talking of a truly valued, loved and capable young man and we will always be very grateful for that.

In our situation, it also helped that the suspicion of Down's syndrome came initially from us and in this way medical staff followed our lead. We were also aware of Sarah's condition very soon after her birth. It thus seemed like a gradual realization through our own awareness as well as the unfolding of clues during Sarah's medical examination on the labour ward. This made the process as gentle as possible.

It is impossible to know exactly how much an individual with Down's syndrome can achieve and no one tried to chart a definite outcome. It was stated that there was a broad range of abilities that Sarah could aspire to and in this way we were left with some hope for the future. Doctors really don't know how each child will develop, they don't know the effect of the various therapies or indeed the environment that the child will grow up in.

Talking to Dr Mackinnon later, she said that in a way she found it easier to break the bad news to us than complete strangers as she had some idea of our reactions. To have to tell parents whom she has possibly never met before that their baby has died or has a major disability understandably remains the most traumatic part of her work. She has many years of experience in these matters and it is frightening to think that this responsibility may be left to a lone junior doctor who has never been in this situation before.

Dr Mackinnon's philosophy when telling parents that their child may have Down's syndrome is to go extremely slowly, allowing the parents to take in what they can at this stage. Awareness of particular cultures, religious views and general philosophy are all vital and yet she is sometimes in a situation where she has never set eyes on these parents before and has no idea how they will respond. In her experience, reactions have ranged from total acceptance, 'We won't love her any more or any less than our other child,' to attempts by one of the parents to kill the newly diagnosed newborn baby.

Dr Mackinnon was even threatened with death by a parent who blamed her for the diagnosis – literally wanting to 'shoot the messenger'. Despite the fact that this particular time of breaking bad news is so significant, she herself received very little training and there is still very little preparation – if any – for junior doctors. Parents are now much more knowledgeable about medical matters, more articulate and much more likely to ask questions about the diagnosis and prognosis. Information is now more readily available and access through journals, parent groups and the Internet creates a much more sophisticated response to vague generalizations about our children.

We were also given a textbook on Down's syndrome, the first chapter of which was entitled 'The first days are the hardest – a bad time for bad news'. Here in black and white was a description of all the emotions that we were going through. It was very reassuring that we weren't in fact going completely round the twist, as it seemed in those dark, early days. It was useful to have something that one could pick up and put down at one's leisure and not be dependent on the availability of busy medical staff. We were told not to read further than the first three chapters and adhered to this obediently. Two years later I realized that I still had not ready any more of the book – you see, I always listen to medical opinion – and when I did eventually continue with the book, the wisdom of the original suggestion became clear. Much of the information and details about the long-term future would have been too much to bear at that stage.

The adage of 'taking one day at a time' may be somewhat of a cliché, but in this case it was the best possible advice.

Of course doctors can never get it completely right – the very nature of the news that they are about to impart makes it impossible for them to judge every situation correctly. There is a likelihood that the parents of a child born with a disability will always be dissatisfied with the way that they are told. There is no easy way to give bad news and mostly, the doctor cannot win. I know of one parent who is still furious that her doctor wasn't more blunt and direct, bemoaning the fact that he was too tactful. She didn't want to hear, 'everything will take your child longer than with an ordinary child, you just mustn't compare him with other children.'

Because this is such a delicate and vital process, the doctor's task is to ensure that he or she is not doing or saying anything to deserve this free-floating anger. It simply cannot be left to the improvisation of one doctor and all clinical staff need careful training and support in this area.

4. There's No Place Like Home

A couple of days after her birth, Sarah was ready to leave hospital. She was still quite jaundiced, but it was agreed that if we kept a careful check on her, she would be able to come home. We departed quietly, with a few words of thanks to the ward staff, but desperately not wanting a big goodbye or a fuss to be made. It was a relief to be out of the hospital and the constant labelling that had marked her arrival. 'What have you got – a boy or a girl?' 'Actually . . . it's a Down's syndrome baby.' It was as if Sarah did not have an identity of her own and wasn't really our baby. She belonged to another extended family, chromosomal cousins called 'the Downses' with their own physical characteristics, their own lifestyle and their own culture. We had somehow unexpectedly inherited this baby from them, but were now expected to raise her as one of our own. She had little hair and what she did have was blonde. She was round faced, snub nosed and almond eyed. She didn't look like us. She was certainly very different from Daniel – unmistakably a product of his parents' genes with his shock of black hair and familial facial features. But this one, well, she didn't really seem to be one of the Merrimans and yet here she was and was now expected to come and live in our house. Perhaps she was just a lodger who wouldn't be staying long – maybe she wouldn't fit in with us and would have to be returned to whence she came.

It was a very subdued homecoming and we really didn't quite know how to behave. It was a bit like New Year's Eve when you know the approaching year is going to be difficult. The event had to be marked – but in what way? We were in no mood for celebrating and yet here was our newborn baby coming home for the first time.

We smuggled her in through the front door as quickly as possible so that the neighbours wouldn't see her and we would all be saved from any difficult doorstep conversations and embarrassing moments.

I had put up a 'Welcome Home, Sarah and Mummy' paper banner in the hallway, which I had hastily made the previous day. Not known for my decorative artwork, it now appeared even more forlorn and tatty and had partly freed itself from the wall, suspended at an oblique angle. The house was so full of tulips, daffodils and carnations that Allie remarked that it resembled a funeral parlour. 'Say it with flowers' is how the slogan reads, but what was the 'it' that friends and family were trying to say?

Every day, following her discharge, Sarah had to be brought back to the Special Care Baby Unit to ascertain that her liver was functioning normally. It was agreed that I would take her back to the hospital each morning for a blood test, as Allie certainly didn't want to face the hospital staff or the rest of the world and I was happy to take on this role, as I felt at least there was something practical that I could do.

The Special Care Baby Unit is an extraordinary place – even for those used to a hospital environment. An outpost of Lilliputian proportion it contains a handful of cots of usual dimension but seeming gigantic in comparison to the miniature babies that they hold. To see those cribs, containing mere scraps of life, resembling skinned rabbits, prematurely dispossessed of the womb and strenuously fighting for existence, is indeed a humbling experience.

I looked at Sarah, who suddenly seemed huge, self-sufficient and much more prepared to do battle. She was free from the tangle of tubes going every which way and of electrodes, monitors, bleeping machines. The bustle of concerned and skilled medical staff, aware of every minute bodily function, surprisingly made me feel more secure. My concern was not for my child's life; she was not ill – not in danger – and yet I could identify with the anxious looks of the parents around me. The arrivals of their babies were no doubt inevitably greeted with drama and fear. All expectation forgotten in the struggle for life. They were probably also living a simultaneous nightmare. The fact that 'ordinary' life was going on in the outside world since Sarah's birth had struck me as strange, but somehow this particularly extraordinary environment made more sense in my current state of heightened emotion and confusion.

The SCBU staff were all incredibly sympathetic and genuinely interested in how we were getting on and I was pleased by the fact that I was being useful and taking an active part in the first week of Sarah's life. However, removing blood from the sole of Sarah's miniature foot seemed somewhat problematic and distressing for her (and me) and after several days, it was decided that I could be trusted with a sort of hand-held metre – a medical instrument that measured Sarah's bilirubin level. (Bilirubin is a yellowish pigment in the bile and excess amounts in the blood produce a jaundiced appearance.) This meant that we would not have to come to hospital and that I could test Sarah at home.

Twice a day, at regular times, I would press the instrument to her forehead with enthusiastic anticipation that the number would continue to come down. In fact I started to make side bets with my dad about each day's figures so that while Sarah's health was improving, I was making money. I also figured that if this was all there was to being a doctor, I should definitely have bothered to attend medical school. The GP who came to visit soon after her arrival was fascinated, as he had never seen this device before. I took great pleasure in explaining to him how it worked. He asked if he could have a go, but I refused, saying that Sarah was my patient and in my view didn't need a second opinion!

Gradually, Sarah's bilirubin level stabilized as her liver started to work effectively and her skin, which had been quite yellow, turned a healthy colour. I reluctantly returned the metre, delighted that Sarah was now 'in the pink', but also realizing that this signalled the end of an extremely promising career in medicine.

The first few weeks after Sarah's homecoming were filled with a regular procession of people, all bearing gifts and helping in every way possible. Between them, friends delivered meals, did the shopping, took Daniel off our hands for a few hours to play and one neighbour even arranged for him to attend her son's playgroup, pushing a double buggy up a steep hill for three days a week. Not only did the immediate family rally round, but friends of friends appeared or telephoned with offers of all sorts of help. A week's supply of home-cooked meals was delivered by an old friend of Allie's and there were many invitations from others, providing understanding, sustenance and good counsel. Friends from all over Britain made the effort to come and see us and we also had a visit from a couple who actually made a day trip from Holland. One of Allie's closest friends, Ruth Lowe, came especially from Philadelphia to be with her. This never-ending fund of assistance helped us to know that we would be able to bring up our new daughter in an atmosphere of love and caring. The feelings of despair that sometimes seemed insurmountable were tempered by the knowledge that our friends were totally understanding of our situation and – more importantly – totally accepting of Sarah.

I know that there is a general criticism of urban life and in particular that Londoners are unfriendly and self-absorbed, but we felt a real sense of community with the help and friendship of neighbours and acquaintances, who just couldn't have done more for us.

In those early days, we were still in a state of shock and felt exhausted and traumatized. We had very little energy and all I can remember doing is collapsing in front of the television in order to distract myself from our horrible reality. I enjoy television. It can be informative, entertaining and therapeutic. I'll watch anything at any time, on any channel and can only marvel at the number of stations I can surf with the remote control. The medium can certainly be more interesting than books – I mean, have you ever tried putting a novel in the corner of the living room and staring at it for hours on end? And when you have young children it is – to borrow the words of Bill Shankly – 'Not a matter of life and death, it's more important than that.'

I am certainly not the sort of parent who dismisses the cathode rays as the cheap and mindless activity of populist culture – well, apart from anything that involves Chris Evans. And so what if it is a distraction which prevents you from making your own entertainment? As far as I'm concerned, if it means a more peaceful life, our kids can watch as much television as they want before the nine o'clock watershed. Having been disturbed from peaceful slumber in the wee small hours and dragged downstairs to a cold kitchen, do you really want to engage your two-year-old with jigsaws and face painting? I don't think so.

I can remember a dark and terrible time in our lives some years ago when the video recorder was broken. I was so desperate at five o'clock one morning that I was actually counting the minutes until the start of the Open University programmes so that Daniel and I would have something to occupy us.

At the time of Sarah's birth, however, the video machine was actually working and Daniel was obsessed with the film, *The Wizard of Oz*. My dad had bought the video for him as a second birthday present and with the obsessive nature that most toddlers possess, he had been watching it almost constantly ever since and thus throughout the latter stages of the pregnancy. We had been treated to the delights of this classic musical at least once a day and our sitting room had become a cinema with the main feature as a continuous performance. This masterpiece was soon to become our *film noir*.

According to one theory, the story is an allegorical tale by Frank Baum concerning a great economic debate about the gold standard (the yellow brick road) that was taking place at the time he wrote the book. Baum tried to highlight the plight of Kansas farmers, who were impoverished by the effects of severe droughts. For us, however, the significance of the film was quite different as it represented something much more personal. It almost became too unbearable to watch when we realized quite how symbolic of our situation the film was turning out to be.

When Dorothy 'arrives' in Munchkinland, she finds herself surrounded by its inhabitants, 'Munchkins', strange ill-formed creatures of midget proportions and odd appearance. They speak with unusual, distorted voices and some are tubby and walk with an ungainly waddle. At that time, we could not help but think of Sarah as a little Munchkin, who wasn't going to be 'normal' like other people and might well have all the characteristics that I have described. She certainly would never be like the little girl as portrayed by Judy Garland – bright, pretty and talented.

Dorothy then follows the yellow brick road in order to find the Wizard, who can help her find her way back to Kansas and to her previous life. Her first encounter along the way is with the Scarecrow. He is perfectly happy with his life except that he would be much better at frightening away birds if he had some intelligence. Dorothy asks him the way to Oz and he points to two different directions. When she tells him to make up his mind, he replies that he can't because he only has straw in his head and admits that he's a failure because he hasn't got a brain.

The man of straw is a loveable, cheerful, happy-go-lucky character of limited intelligence and seemed to sum up the stereotypical view of a person with Down's syndrome.

Continuing on their quest, Dorothy, Toto and the Scarecrow

stumble upon the Tin Man, who was caught in a rainstorm whilst chopping wood, became 'rusted solid' and has been unable to move for a year. Once Dorothy has applied oil to his joints, he is able to communicate and use his limbs once more. Dorothy tells the Tin Man that he is now 'perfect' to which he replies he isn't at all perfect because if she bangs on his chest she will discover that the tinsmith forgot to give him a heart.

Sarah was diagnosed as having a hole in her heart and would need to be under the regular care of a heart specialist. It was possible that this hole would close naturally and that she might not need surgery, but it was obviously of great concern to us and yet another worry for her future.

The third character Dorothy meets along the way is in a sinister, dark forest where she and her new-found friends are terrified by the thought of meeting 'lions and tigers and bears'. They do meet a lion, but he is frightened by Dorothy when he tries to attack Toto. He is the Cowardly Lion, who needs courage.

If there was ever a time when Allie and I found overselves in a dark, gloomy and frightening place, this was it and there was no doubt that we were going to need a lot of courage to overcome the 'lions and tigers and bears' of life.

Dorothy reaches the Emerald City, where the Wizard lives, only to be refused entry by the gatekeeper. When, however, she states that the Good Witch of the North has sent her, he uses the expression, 'Well, that's a horse of a different colour.' Dorothy and the others are then allowed in and are driven through the streets of the city by horse and carriage. The horse is originally white, then turns pink, purple, red and yellow.

Even this scene had some significance for us in that 'the horse of a different colour' also appeared to describe how we felt about Sarah. She was something different, a variation on a theme, something that wasn't quite the standard issue.

The song 'Over the Rainbow' is supposedly symbolic of many

people's dreams and our dreams at that time had been shattered. The lyrics were also significant:

> *Someday I'll wish upon a star,*
> *And wake up where the clouds are far behind me,*
> *Where troubles melt like lemon drops,*
> *Way up above the chimney tops,*
> *That's where you'll find me.*

It seemed impossible in those dark days that we would ever find a magical place where our troubles could just melt away and I must say that at that time, we were no friends of Dorothy's.

5. Letter From America

Within a week of Sarah's birth, we received a letter which was to have a profound effect on our ability to come to terms with the reality of our situation. Ken Hixon is a screen-writer based in Hollywood and, although we had never met, we shared a mutual friend. Sarah's godfather, Paul Kelly, had telephoned Ken and his wife Melanie immediately with our news.

13 January 1992/Los Angeles

Dear Ally and Andrew,

My name is Ken Hixon, I am the father of Lilian Hixon, who happens to be one of my most noteworthy accomplishments. Lily is eight years old, a girl of extraordinary will, affection, humour and beauty, and lower on the list with her other vital statistics would be the notation 'Down syndrome'.

Not that it isn't obvious that Lily has Down syndrome, indeed she has all the characteristics, but what strikes people first and foremost about Lily is her joyful and amazing personality. I'm certain my bias is quite blatant by now. But beyond my bond to her as father to child, as a somewhat eccentric person myself, and married to a woman of distinct individuality, what draws me so tightly to Lily is her utter uniqueness. She is one of the most original people I've ever met.

She is fearless, but astutely sensitive. She is clumsy, but innately poised. She is an anarchist with a Zen-like zeal for ritual and routine. I think the word is contradictions. An apt word for Lily

47

and for many of the feelings and experiences her mother and I have had.

To say that giving birth to a child with Down Syndrome was a painful shock is, as you already know, a sublime understatement. But graced as we were by the affections of our friends and family, the level headed advice of our paediatrician, and our own stamina and love for each other, my wife, Melanie, and I rose, somewhat wobbly, to the challenge at hand. Not without pain nor tears, not without insecurities and confusion. But simply. The best advice we received early on was just to take our new baby home and enjoy her. That there is ample time to become experts on mental retardation. We learned the wisdom of this immediately. We just took a breath and found that Lily's needs were no more complex than any other infant's — she needed to be fed, bathed, changed, hugged, kissed, held, and made funny faces at. In fact after just a few months I decided that if Lily is retarded then I must be retarded as well because she made perfect sense to me.

Her so-called 'slow' development was just my speed. In fact after the birth of our son, Sam, we labelled him 'severely normal'. Indeed, it would be a toss-up determining which child has placed the most demands on us as parents. Of course I don't mean to brush aside the enormous amount of energy and effort to meet the needs of a child with Down Syndrome. And I certainly do not wish to infer that I have no concern for the social 'slings and arrows' Lilian will suffer in this oh so perfect world. I do worry. I do get depressed. I am anxious at times, but most of the time, the overwhelming majority of the time, I am just in love with Lily.

I would be lost without her.

All my best

Ken Hixon

Allie and I were both incredibly moved by the letter – not just the beautifully written content, but by the efficiency with which the network had begun to spread the news and the speed with which Ken had composed and posted this missive. Lily, a complete stranger 6,000 miles away, had entered our lives in the same way that our own daughter had done a few days earlier. Was it really possible that Sarah could achieve what Lily had achieved in only eight years? Could Sarah become a similar character – an individual, full of potential and with her own unique personality?

It also touched us that this couple – unknown to us until this letter – had faced the very same situation eight years previously and had survived the ordeal. The family seemed to be so very different from the image that I kept thinking of – a family burdened by the addition of a disabled child, struggling from one crisis to the next and unable to lead a 'normal' life. This family seemed to be alive, full of joy, whilst acknowledging the difficulties. They were optimistic about the future, but not mindlessly impervious to the troubles that would evolve from time to time.

And as for Lily – well, we just loved her already. Despite the fact that we had never met her, we were completely smitten. Maybe we could fall in love with our own daughter sometime in the future. If Ken and Melanie could discover so much love for Lily, then why couldn't we?

Allie carried this letter everywhere and read it constantly for the first month after Sarah's birth. It became a sort of Down's syndrome passport, 'allowing the bearer to pass freely without let or hindrance and to afford the bearer such assistance and protection as may be necessary'. We could venture into unknown territory and unexplored lands with this document and it would also enable the bearer to discuss the subject of Down's syndrome at any time with any person. The letter would be produced in a flash and thrust upon any friend, acquaintance or member of the public who had unwittingly shown even a passing interest. Supermarket shoppers idly checking the 'Kosher Korner' for a deal on sweet cucumbers or chopped herring and who paused for a moment to smile at Sarah would receive a five-minute lecture on special needs and a copy of the letter.

Following Sarah's cardiac scan at the Whittington, she was then referred to an eminent paediatric heart specialist and instead of handing him the referral letter from Dr Mackinnon, Allie, by mistake, handed him Ken Hixon's letter. He read it for a couple of minutes, becoming more and more puzzled until he handed us back the letter and said, 'Lily seems like a nice girl, but what is this to do with me?' I am still convinced that he only realized it wasn't a letter from another doctor because he could read the writing.

I had the opportunity to meet the Hixon family the following summer when I visited California. I had actually lived in Los Angeles for a year in the early 1980s and amongst other jobs sold sandwiches in Santa Monica. My clientele ranged from the beatifically smiling healers at the Acupressure Workshop (avocado and alfalfa sprouts on wholewheat), to an English secretary employed in a theatrical agency (Cheddar cheese on white). I used to trudge up the endless stairway (the walls festooned with photographs of the proprietor) to the opulent office of Arnold Schwarzenegger (turkey, Swiss cheese, coleslaw on sourdough) and then on to Evelyn Winkler at the Shell Shop, chatting to her friend, Mario Puzo. 'He'll take a chopped liver on rye – so what if he's not Jewish?'

The Zsa-Zsa lookalike at Pacific Realtors (egg salad on pumpernickel bread) approached me most days with the question, 'Would you like to buy a piece of property?' 'Yes of course,' I replied, 'as soon as I've sold all my sandwiches, I'll be back with a deposit for a beach front residence in Malibu.' The last stop on the route meant that I had to step out of the glorious warmth of the sunshine and descend into the dark and gloomy confines of the Pink Elephant bar. I went in there dutifully every day for a whole year and I didn't sell a single sandwich. 'Oh no, we don't want to buy anything – we just want to hear your accent.'

I loved living in Los Angeles. By day, a city mainly bereft of beauty, but by night an illuminated, shimmering wonderland. Surrounded by natural splendour and within two hours of barren desert, snow-capped mountains and the Pacific Ocean. OK, there may be some truth in the fact that there's more culture in yoghurt than in Los Angeles, but in terms of cinema, music and fringe theatre, there is certainly no shortage. The city is naturally dominated by the movie industry and everybody has an acting, writing or directing deal that is 'pending', 'about to happen', 'close to realization' or 'virtually in production', an abundance of both unfettered ego and undiscovered talent. There's a wonderful *New Yorker* cartoon, in which a couple are sitting at a table in an LA restaurant and the man, wanting some service, clicks his fingers and calls out, 'Actor!'

I've thus always enjoyed returning to California, as it has always felt like my second home, but this particular trip to meet the Hixons was much more significant. I had made contact with Melanie on my arrival and it transpired that Lily was participating in the Californian Special Olympics the same weekend. Melanie asked me if I wanted to go to the opening ceremony with them, but warned me that the experience might be a bit daunting. I said that I would very much like to go and we arranged to meet at their apartment.

It was strange walking into the home of complete strangers and seeing a picture of your own family on their fridge. Ken and Melanie were incredibly welcoming and it was wonderful to meet Lily and her younger brother Sam. Lily was just how Ken had described her and she was particularly inquisitive about Sarah. I was terribly moved by Lily's interest in Sarah, who was by then just eighteen months old. Although they were separated by age, culture and were two completely different characters, they already shared a common bond. Ken remarked to me later that having a child with Down's syndrome was a bit like being part of the Volkswagen Association. 'Welcome. You're now part of the club. We all have our own models of varying ages and colour, with distinctive specifications, each going at a different pace. You're going to spend a lot of time talking about your particular prototype, but you'll want to know how all the other members are getting on.'

The drive from West Hollywood to the Westwood campus of University of California was fairly short and Lily, although a little nervous about her forthcoming competition, chattered excitedly. When she did pause for breath, Melanie managed to explain about the Special Olympics. Founded in 1968 by Eunice Kennedy Shriver, the Special Olympics provides year round training and athletic competition for more than one million athletes in nearly 150 countries. It is a non-profit, international programme for individuals with learning disability and the intention is that not only do the competitors improve physical fitness and motor skills, develop greater self-confidence and a more positive self-image, but that important friendships are formed and nurtured.

Worldwide, more than 500,000 volunteers, acting as coaches, officials and drivers, give their time and are part of the process to create a greater understanding of the needs and capabilities of the learning disabled.

We arrived at the campus and parked. As we got out of the car, Lily's best friend Jessica rushed up to her and gave her a huge hug. Jessica and Lily were both representing Los Angeles County and were apparently inseparable. They couldn't wait to get away from us to join their coach and other team-mates and after bidding us an excited farewell ran off on to the track.

We walked slowly towards the enormous stadium and I was aware that Melanie was carefully watching for my reactions. She gave me an affectionate hug and asked me if I was all right. She wondered if I was really ready for this experience and her concern was well founded. I was overwhelmed. For not only were we surrounded by thousands and thousands of parents, friends, relations, volunteers and helpers, but we were also enveloped by thousands of adults and children with learning disabilities and huge numbers of them had Down's syndrome.

I'm afraid to say that I couldn't take my eyes off them.

Would Sarah look like this girl behind me or that young woman over there? Is that how she'll walk? Is that how her hair might be? Would she talk like that teenager? Would she be the shape of that middle-aged woman? I had to remind myself that Sarah was only a toddler and what I was doing would be unthinkable in any other situation.

There was no way that I would look at a group of dark-haired teenagers and wonder how Daniel might compare. But then these people all shared a common identity and it was not mine or Allie's. This aspect of their identity was the same, but their differences were even more marked.

I thought of my small daughter back home in London and desperately wanted her to be with me. I felt that if she were, I could focus more clearly on Sarah as her own little being and not enmesh her individuality in a group identity. I found it difficult to hold back the tears as several of the athletes spoke to the assembled crowd of their hopes and aspirations not only for these games, but also for their future lives. It was also highly emotional when the Olympic flame, which had been run in relay from San Francisco by the Californian State Police, was carried into the arena in turn by three athletes. The moment was only lightened when one of the runners – a young man with Down's syndrome – happened to run the wrong way and was last seen sprinting out of the stadium in the direction of Santa Monica.

The competitors representing the various Californian counties – all carrying flags and banners and sporting their particular team colours – paraded around the magnificent arena. In true Los Angeles style, show business played a big part, for each group was accompanied by a television or film celebrity. Over the incredibly impressive sound system, the commentator would announce the respective teams.

'And now, led by Steve Schlemiel, star of the popular television soap, *Day of Our Wives*, is the Sonoma County team. Let's have a big hand for the team and especially for Steve – soon to be seen in a major motion picture, due for release in the fall, *Robo Nannies Shrunk My Baby*.'

The opening ceremony ended with fireworks, music and general razzmatazz that the Americans do so well. The next day the games would begin and Lily and Jessica would be ready to do their best for themselves and their team-mates. I hoped that one day, Sarah would benefit from the devoted and loyal friendship of a Lily or a Jessica and that she, too, might be involved in this sort of event.

The spirit of the Special Olympics, the skill, courage, sharing, and joy transcend boundaries of geography, nationality, political philosophy, gender, age, race, or religion. The motto, 'Let me win. But if I cannot win, let me be brave in the attempt' seems to me to be a perfect maxim for Sarah. I know that society might not view Sarah as a winner, but she must have the right to compete on her own terms and she must – and we must – be brave . . .

6. Idiocy of a Mongolian Type

I can't stand anything N.P.A. Non-Physically Attractive. Old
women in bathing-suits – and skin diseases – and cripples . . .
Rowton House-looking men who spit and have hair growing out
of their ears . . . No good, I just can't look at them . . . One –
place – we went, there were these poor freaks with – oh, you
know – enormous heads and so on – and you just feel: oh, put
them out of their misery. Well, they wouldn't have survived in
nature, it's only modern medicine so modern medicine should
be allowed to do away with them. A committee of doctors and
do-gooders, naturally, to make sure there's no funny business
and then – if I say gas-chamber that makes it sound horrid – but
I do mean put to sleep.

An extract from the play, *A Day in the Death of Joe Egg* by
Peter Nichols, which was first performed at the Citizens'
Theatre in Glasgow in 1967 and met with universal acclaim as
one of the most touching, original and funny pieces ever written
about disability. A black comedy that was considered ground
breaking at the time and which remains timeless.

Down's syndrome has probably existed for about ten million
years – as long as humankind – but 'idiocy of a mongolian type'
is first described in a book published in 1844 and there are a
couple of earlier references to Down's syndrome in the previous
decade.

According to Brian Stratford in his book, '*Down's Syndrome,
Past, Present and Future*, the Athenians and Spartans deserted
handicapped babies on hillsides to starve or be taken by wild

animals. In Greek culture the handicapped were not considered to be human, but 'monsters' belonging to a different species. In fifth century Athens, 'democracy' only extended to the 'public' people – men – whilst slaves, women and the handicapped were not involved in civic matters and were therefore 'private' people. The Greek word for a private person is 'idiots' and the word 'idiot' was still being used as a medical term of severely handicapped people in the early 1970s. The word is obviously still in use, but only as a term of insult.

Even Martin Luther, the sixteenth century social reformer, called for the burning of the mother and handicapped child – obviously the result of fornication with the devil, and this notion of moral depravity lasted well into the middle of this century.

In the 1860s, the first large-scale institution was built in order to incarcerate and segregate people then known as 'idiots' and 'the insane' together in large numbers. Its chief physician was Langdon Down, who was the first person to accurately describe the syndrome which bears his name. Strongly influenced by Darwin, he appeared to regard the retarded as evolutionary throwbacks to inferior races and he classified idiots in terms of ethnicity. He claimed to identify 'Negroid' and 'Malayan' types and he named the syndrome 'mongolism' because of the Mongoloid appearance of the eyes.

R. Chambers in his book, *The Vestiges of the Natural History of Creation*, which was published in 1844, states, 'The Mongolian, Malay, American and Negro, comprehending perhaps five-sixths of mankind are degenerate.'

In other words, the degenerate behaviour is based on race not personality or lack of intelligence. In addition to being influenced by these somewhat dubious theories, Down was also of the opinion that alcoholism and tuberculosis were also causes of 'mongolism'. It was not until 1959 that Professor Jerome Lejeune identified the extra chromosome as being the cause of Down's syndrome and with this breakthrough came the possibility of diagnosing a whole range of genetic disorders.

Meanwhile, the degeneracy of the 'lower orders' was blamed for the numbers of 'moral defectives' and there was little that could be done for these particular groups of 'unfortunates'. There was no chance of a 'cure' or a likely change in their behaviour and, of course, the public had to be protected. E. R. Johnstone, the President of the American Association of Mental Deficiency at the turn of this century, called for 'institutional care as a method of elimination' for those who showed 'arrested or incomplete development of the mind . . . as it shocks no-one's ideas of propriety, humanity and Christianity'. He had previously rejected the 'unsexing' of these people as it might not have found favour with the public.

In 1927, Oliver Wendell Holmes – the American Supreme Court Judge – declared in a test case that involuntary sterilization was 'constitutional'.

> We have seen more than once that the public welfare may call upon the best citizens for their lives. It would be strange if it could not call upon those who already sap the strength of the state for these lesser sacrifices, often not felt to be such by those concerned, in order to prevent being swamped with incompetence. It is better for all the world if, instead of waiting to execute degenerate offspring for their crime, or to let them starve for their imbecility, society can prevent those who are manifestly unfit from continuing their kind. The principle that sustains compulsory vaccination is broad enough to cover cutting the Fallopian tubes . . . Three generations of imbeciles is enough.

This view was later compounded by the German government, who in 1934 passed legislation which sanctioned the compulsory sterilization of the congenitally feeble-minded. Within a few years, over 400,000 Germans were sterilized – about one in every hundred of its population.

This was, of course, only the beginning. Between 1939 and 1945, the Nazis carried out a euthanasia programme in which over 200,000 mentally ill, mentally handicapped and physically disabled people and over 6,000 children were killed. Described as 'life unworthy as life', they were systematically incarcerated, segregated and then killed by various means – but usually by starvation.

This was not driven by a medical agenda, but purely on an economic basis. The cost of keeping an 'incurable idiot' in an increasingly market-led economy was a waste of money. It is also true to say that most people were actually placed in asylums by their own families – not only influenced by financial reasons, but also no doubt influenced by the ideology and by the stigma of familial impurity.

Michael Burleigh in his fascinating book, *Death and Deliverance*, states, 'the euthanasia programme was a carefully planned and covertly executed operation with precisely defined objectives . . . Mentally and physically disabled people were killed to save money and resources.'

Within sight of one such institution, Sonnenstein, near Dresden, where nearly 14,000 'mentally retarded' people were gassed and cremated, Sarah's grandmother, Ursula Hess, was living with her sister, Luise, and their parents. Her father was a research chemist who owned a paint factory and her mother an accomplished pianist.

Ursula went to the local secondary school until Jews were banned from attendance and she then attended a Jewish school in nearby Dresden. On the morning of 9 November 1938, her father was taken away to the local prison (to be transferred later to the Buckenwald concentration camp) and that night – the infamous 'Kristallnacht' – a mob of several hundred stormed the family home. Ursula, then aged thirteen, her sister, and mother took refuge on the staircase leading to the cellar and although there was some damage to the building and personal belongings, the terrified family escaped unharmed. That night, under the cover of darkness, the three of them went to stay with relatives in Dresden.

They were never to return to live in their home and the two daughters left for England in June of 1939. Ursula's father was released from Buchenwald and with his wife managed to obtain passports a week before war broke out. A number of their family did not, however, manage to escape and perished in the Theresienstadt and Auschwitz concentration camps. Allie's father, John Wellemin, who was born in Prague, also fled to England before the war and many more of his family were wiped out by the Nazis. John returned to Prague with the Czech army after the war, but escaped from the Communists in 1948 and eventually settled in England where he met Ursula at a language school.

I cannot help but think what would have happened to Sarah if she had been born in Germany during that period. As a 'mental defective' or as 'life unworthy of life', would she have been part of the children's euthanasia programme or would she somehow have survived this only to become another Jewish victim of 'The Final Solution'?

Although the subject of pre-natal testing is something that I will address in greater detail later in the book, there is an obvious link between this horrific era, in what is, historically, a relatively recent epoch, and the current genetic 'advances' designed to wipe out those who do not quite fit our idea of 'normal'.

Normality is, of course, a subjective concept. Everyone's idea of normal behaviour or activity is different and cannot really be defined. Being described as a normal person may not exactly be the stuff that dreams are made of, but then being described as a 'mongoloid idiot' is neither subjective nor acceptable.

As I have already stated, this term as a medical diagnosis was still very much in use less than thirty years ago and derived from earlier legislation. In Britain, the 1866 Idiots Act made a clear distinction between 'lunatics' and 'born fools' and by 1870 the Education Act subdivided the whole range, the criterion being the educability of the various grades of 'defect'. The Mental Deficiency Act of 1913 included the three established levels of retardation: idiot, imbecile and feeble-minded.

There is no doubt that the use of particular language and terminology throughout history has had a huge influence on the way that people with Down's syndrome and indeed other disabilities have been treated. An inextricable link exists between legislation, words and social policy and the attempts at using language that is less pejorative can only help in the understanding of disability.

Sarah Boston's very moving book, *Will, My Son*, written in 1981, recounts the story of her son, Will, who had Down's syndrome, and who died at the age of eight months. In her sequel, *Too Deep For Tears*, which was written to mark what would have been Will's eighteenth birthday, she addresses the subject of language and terminology. She states, 'Language reflects our feelings and our attitudes . . . it is an outward and visible symbol,' and goes on to stress the importance that terminology plays in the way that we treat people. I cannot agree more as I believe that any change in words or idiom reflect the changes in our thinking.

The argument that language is not important is, I believe, misplaced and the arrogant and condescending dismissal of certain words or terms as 'politically correct' and therefore supposedly a source of amusement is extremely annoying. Terminology is meaningful and should not be dismissed as being trite and unimportant. It also does not mean that because time and energy is expended on this issue that other important battles of equality in education or employment are forgotten. It is the same battle.

Of course one can always quote examples where the theory has gone too far, but this is not the point. 'Idiots', 'cretins', 'morons', 'imbeciles', 'half-wits' and 'fools' have all been used to describe children and people with learning difficulties. I remember at school boys were often described as 'mongols', if they acted in a silly way or 'spassies' if they weren't physically very adept. I don't suppose these contemptuous remarks would have held the same edge if we had been insulted with, 'You stupid child with learning difficulties' or 'You pathetic cerebral palsy sufferer!'

I realize that 'learning difficulties' is not ideal because I am well aware that Sarah's difficulties amount to much more than those of 'learning', but this term and 'learning disabled' is how adults in this situation wish to be described. These terms are certainly more acceptable than 'mental defective' or 'retard' and 'handicapped' with the connotation of street corner begging and charity handouts.

Even when I first started in social work in the mid-1970s, people with Down's syndrome were still described as 'mongols' and all people with learning difficulties were described as 'sub-normal'. And worse, they were categorized into 'high' and 'low' grade. I'm afraid that the description of such clients as 'subbies' was much in evidence and I was as guilty as anyone else in this regard. I would be outraged if anyone used that term when describing Sarah – and I should have been outraged then . . .

Despite all this, I don't want to get too strident about the subject and although I don't like Sarah being described as a 'Down's child' – she is Sarah first and foremost – I have to say that I don't have the same adverse reaction as some other parents. I understand completely why some parents are also unhappy when their child is described as a 'victim of' or 'suffering from' Down's syndrome and although I tend not to use this kind of phrase because of its negative connotations, it doesn't enrage me. This is probably because I feel rather mixed about this specific concept.

Certainly, objectively, Sarah's mental and physical capabilities are limited. It is not just that she cannot 'perform' as society expects – she also cannot achieve things as quickly and effectively as she would like. For instance, at times her memory lets her down, but then she passes this off with a 'Silly me!' and tries again seeming not to mind that she is not as sharp as her friends. Perhaps, too, in PE at school she is suffering due to the fact that she cannot jump as high as or skip like the others, but this doesn't seem to affect her. 'PE today!' Sarah punches the air. 'I love it!'

Maybe Sarah doesn't see herself as a 'victim' at this stage of her life, but when she is faced by the fact that, for example, due to a chromosomal disorder she might not be able to have children, she might well feel victimized. We can only hope that she will feel so accepting of who she is and how loved she is by those dear to her, that any objective limitations facing her will feel surmountable.

7. An Earful of Cider

It was the middle of January. Sarah had been home for about ten days and needed an all-in-one outdoor outfit. I agreed to go and buy one and drove to the local shopping centre. This whole trip shouldn't take me more than forty-five minutes – I was quite decisive about this sort of thing and often bought the first item that caught my eye.

I parked in the multi-storey car park and wandered down to a big store, which specialized in baby and toddler clothing. I looked at the rows of garments and stood, considering the choices before me. What size would she need? Of course, there was no point in buying for a newborn baby as she would grow out if it quite quickly. But then again, she's got Down's syndrome and so she won't grow so fast. Now . . . what about the colour? Does it matter? Of course it does. I mustn't buy something garish which might draw particular attention to her . . . I wouldn't want that. But then I couldn't possibly choose a delicate shade because . . . well . . . she's unlikely to be petite or dainty. Pink was definitely out, because I didn't want anything 'girly' and I couldn't possibly buy anything in blue, as it would just be making an unnecessary political point for its own sake. Black was too funereal – I was already feeling depressed enough as it was – and white was virginal and impractical.

What about the expense? I couldn't buy anything too cheap, because then it might be assumed that I couldn't care less what Sarah wore and didn't value her enough. But then again, if I bought something too expensive, then I would merely be over-compensating and this would be equally wrong. Oh dear, this was getting difficult. No, it was no good, there was obviously nothing I could buy in this shop – I had better try elsewhere.

I went into another half a dozen outlets, but with each shop my decision became harder and harder and I became more and more confused. With every new store, the level of anxiety grew. This was ridiculous – what could be more straightforward than buying some clothing for my daughter? But this was becoming increasingly complicated and turning into something much more significant than I realized.

In one shop, I confided in a shop assistant and rambled on for what seemed ages about the situation and my personal dichotomy. She was extremely nice and helpful, but I'm sure didn't comprehend what I was talking about. In another shop, I became quite annoyed when the assistant was only able to show me one outfit. 'Just because she's got Down's syndrome doesn't mean I shouldn't have some choice for her.' The poor woman looked completely bemused as I trudged out of the shop, feeling absolutely desperate.

My shopping expedition finally came to an end when I entered a shop and saw a young woman with Down's syndrome packing shelves with children's underwear. I stopped in my tracks and stared at her – not caring if she noticed me or other people saw what I was doing. Is this what Sarah was destined for? Would this be the most she might achieve in a working capacity? Is this as much as we could hope for? And yet . . . she might never even be able to do this menial work. This sort of job might well be beyond Sarah's capabilities when she grew up. What on earth did the future hold?

I hurried back to the car and drove the short distance home in floods of tears. I went into the house to Allie and her mother, who happened to be visiting. I could hardly speak. 'I'm sorry, but I couldn't do it . . . I couldn't get her outfit. I'm sorry . . . I'm really sorry.'

Poor Ursula had never seen me so upset and I felt very

embarrassed that such a simple task had resulted in such an outpouring of emotion. Of course, we all knew that I wasn't just crying about a coat and the reason for my tears was much more profound, but it did seem so pathetic at the time. After half an hour of explanation, tea and sympathy, I decided – like falling off a horse – I had to go out and try again. I went to another part of town and finally purchased this much sought-after garment – it would have been easier to find a Gucci original.

I had virtually spent the whole day searching for one piece of clothing for Sarah and I wondered that if this was how life was going to continue, how on earth we would have time for any other family activity? Supposing we wanted to buy her a bicycle when she's older – I'd have to set aside a whole year for that task.

This particular day was one of the most depressing and upsetting of the whole period since Sarah's birth. A supposedly simple act had manifested into a major traumatic event and symbolized all the ambivalent and ambiguous feelings that I had about Sarah. I was naturally still very bewildered and soon realized that the only way that I could manage was to try to return to the 'normal' routine. I was anxious to get back to work and try and pick up the pieces of ordinary life. I wasn't trying to avoid the situation. How could I possibly do that? It was a method of coping with the shock and the future ahead. I talked to my friends and family at great length, but I am by nature quite stoical and I am not a worrier. All right . . . so maybe I was reacting in a typically male way, but this was how it was. Unlike Allie, I didn't need to discuss endlessly every scenario from every possible angle. I just wanted to get on with it and for these first, terrible few weeks to be over. Sarah was here and we somehow just had to manage. Sarah's arrival had been a fluke. A case of what appeared to be poor fortune.

In *The Idyll of Miss Sarah Brown* by Damon Runyon, a father gives advice to his son, who is leaving his small home town in

Colorado. The son, nicknamed 'The Sky' because of his expansive betting habits, is leaving to seek fame and fortune in the big wide world. The old man tells him:

> 'no matter how far you travel, or how smart you get, always remember this: Someday, somewhere, a guy is going to come to you and show you a nice new deck of cards on which the seal is never broken, and this guy is going to offer to bet you that the jack of spades will jump out of this deck and squirt cider in your ear. But, son,' the old guy says, 'do not bet him, for as sure as you do, you are going to get an earful of cider.'

In the first few months after Sarah's birth, we felt that our ears were dripping with cider. With the odds of having a baby with Down's syndrome at somewhere in the region of 600 to one it seemed that this was more than somewhat of a sucker bet. The chance that these odds should come up was unbelievable and yet it had happened. Even Sky Masterson would have been astounded.

It was ironic because Allie and I had always considered ourselves lucky. We had both experienced happy, stable childhoods and our families were well and financially comfortable. Up until the shock of Sarah's birth, we had led fairly charmed lives. Perhaps we had become too smug, too arrogant in our security and this was how we were being repaid. Was it really bad luck or divine retribution? At the time it didn't seem to matter. I was too upset, too confused to think about it and soon . . . too busy.

Within the first month or two, there seemed to be a huge succession of helpers and callers and the constant activity of visitors and telephone calls helped to distract us and enable us to survive. The immediate reactions of our families could not have been better. Allie's sister, Carey, was a great source of support – she was always happy to listen to Allie and offered sound and sensible advice. She undertook her sisterly duties with great sensitivity. She was also faced with the added burden of adapting to her own role as an aunt of a child with Down's syndrome and all the changing emotions and responsibilities. Being the older sister imbued her with a lifelong protectiveness which was cemented by this experience.

I have read and heard of grandparents of babies with Down's syndrome, whose own outdated views and negative feelings have been their main preoccupation and have therefore created further pressures on an already struggling family. Our parents seemed to approach the situation with uniform acceptance. There was never an expressed doubt about whether we would or should keep Sarah and any secret fears were kept tightly under wraps. The focus for each of the four parents was simply to help us cope in any way that was required and this was a tremendous relief to both of us.

Allie's mother's weekly visits became her most important emotional prop. Fortunately for me, Allie could empty herself of all her thoughts and feelings and did not feel she was burdening her mother, which she felt she was often doing with her close friends. This closeness was further enhanced by the fact that Ursula's feelings mirrored Allie's. The mutual understanding was total.

Allie had to talk about all aspects of the situation from every possible angle – an unending stream of consciousness, worries, concerns, possibilities and likely and unlikely scenarios that had to be explored, dissected and then reassembled for further discussion. Every thought was expressed, no idea left unsaid. Allie was desperate to find a reason for Sarah's existence and was in turmoil. The moment of conception was the key to it all.

Sarah was conceived in Suffolk. Allie wondered whether we had been too close to the Sizewell 'B' nuclear reactor, which blotted out the beautiful coastal landscape in the area. She dwelt on all the circumstances relating to the moment of conception:

had the quarrel that she and I had had somehow tainted the atmosphere and destroyed any prospect of a happy outcome? If we hadn't argued, would there have been an earlier moment of conception and ultimately a different baby? Allie obsessed on and on about this and other possibilities *ad infinitum*!

We had always operated very differently on an emotional level, but this was now a time of crisis and we had to respect each other's coping mechanisms more seriously than ever before. We had to strike up a pact. Allie had to channel her outpourings through other outlets. I just couldn't handle this constant emotional barrage and it was making me feel more miserable, frustrated and helpless.

I understood that Allie was working her way through the grief by talking about Sarah constantly, but it was having the adverse effect on me. I had actually accepted Sarah for who she was amazingly quickly and needed now to try and take stock of the situation and look to the immediate future – one day at a time. I felt that I had to try and hold the family together, but Allie's need to talk all the time about 'what might have been' was making me feel more depressed.

Of course, Allie had to have the opportunity to talk about the situation as much as she wanted and I didn't want to deny her this need. She had to visit friends, have people over, spend as much time and money on the telephone as she wanted. She had to attend as many self-help groups and meetings as she wanted, but I couldn't be involved at every turn. I also wanted to talk about the situation, but I just wasn't capable of devoting as much time and energy to all the whys and wherefores that Allie could.

It was amazing that we ever made it out of the house in those first few weeks what with all the talking that went on and Allie did actually find the thought of having Sarah observed and commented on very difficult. This was not made any easier by a remark made by a friend of Allie's, who had never met Sarah.

He obviously felt it important to speak the unspeakable and during a telephone conversation he asked, 'Do you feel like covering her face when you go out?'

Our first trip out as a family foursome was to the local shops to buy bunk beds for the children. Daniel was in a buggy and I carried Sarah in a sling. We might have appeared the 'perfect' family and indeed a woman actually remarked as much to us. This image seemed so far from the truth and belied the family turmoil. We just wanted to retreat back to the privacy of our home and shut out everyone who didn't know the pain we were going through.

We were so distracted and disordered during this shopping trip that we ended up buying the first beds we saw – far too big for their room. To this day, the bunks extend too far along the wall and actually prevent anyone opening the bedroom door properly – a daily reminder of the confusion of those early days.

When we did take Sarah out in those first few weeks, we dreaded being stopped by people whose natural inclination was to bill and coo and ask all the usual questions about a newborn baby. I'm sure that people who didn't know us probably had no idea that Sarah had Down's syndrome, but we were absolutely convinced that it was on their minds and they just didn't want to say anything that might upset us.

Thus, complete strangers who happened to glance in Sarah's direction would be accosted and advised of Sarah's name, age and diagnosis – whether they were interested or not. Confession was the handshake. Passers-by, who thought that they were merely passing by, were prevented from doing so and given a ten-minute lecture on our situation. The faintest of smiles in our direction was the cue for a discussion on children with learning disabilities and the implications therein. No pedestrian was safe from Allie's watchful eye, should one show the slightest inclination to make comment on our second-born.

However, after a while, it dawned on us that people probably didn't even notice that Sarah looked different from other babies and that even if they were aware of her having Down's syndrome, they were probably not interested enough to endure a long conversation. We were completely obsessed and I'm afraid everyone we came into contact with at that time must have got really fed up with us.

As I've stated previously, Sarah was diagnosed at birth as having a heart problem, but she needed a more detailed electrocardiogram to ascertain the exact nature and seriousness and she was thus referred to the Royal Brompton Hospital. Strangely enough, we weren't particularly nervous about this appointment, which was exactly two weeks after her birth. Life seemed to be so fraught with difficulty already, the possibility of a potential operation or further medical treatment seemed almost insignificant in light of Sarah's future emotional needs.

I remember that our appointment was delayed by about two hours, owing to an emergency in the hospital and whilst we were waiting to be seen, we saw a middle-aged couple with a baby boy of about nine months. He was the first child with Down's syndrome we had encountered since Sarah's birth and the effect upset us both greatly and bore out all our fears for the future. The baby was thin, pale and withdrawn. The mother appeared exhausted, haggard and depressed and the father, bored and miserable. A sort of Arthur Mullard and Rita Webb in the making. They sat listlessly together, hardly communicating with each other or the child and seemed unaware of the environment or our scrutiny. I wondered if the coming months were going to take a similar toll on us and we would soon be looking as aged and depressed. Could our relationship possibly withstand the strain and pressure that was inevitably to affect us?

We were finally led into the consulting room to be faced with a mountain of technological instruments and banks of electrocardiogram machines. Naturally our hearts sank at the thought of our tiny Sarah being wired up to and at the mercy of all this technology. Amazingly, the consultant ignored these appliances, preferring to diagnose Sarah's condition by just using a stethoscope. He listened to the various rumblings and gurglings of her heart with the concentration and intensity of a man conducting an orchestra. His junior doctor, trembling with excitement at the thought of employing all the modern machinery at his disposal, seemed almost disappointed by this. Finally, the consultant reluctantly agreed to let his junior have his way and with the relish of a young Dr Frankenstein, the medic hooked Sarah up!

An ASD (Atrial Septal Defect) was confirmed later, meaning that Sarah had a hole in the wall separating the two atria. It was explained that this is common in children with Down's syndrome and should not have any permanent effect on her life or her life expectancy. With luck, the hole would close naturally in due course and surgery would probably not be required.

Of course, in retrospect, if Sarah's heart condition had been serious, it would have caused us much more worry and all our lives would have been further altered by this additional burden. The prospect of leading a 'normal' family life in the future would have been far more remote, as we would have been embroiled in a flurry of hospital appointments and procedures. Sarah's progress would have been further delayed and there would have been even less time to devote to Daniel.

Nearly five years later, the same specialist in the same consulting room in the Brompton confirmed that the hole in Sarah's heart had actually closed by itself. We walked away from the hospital for the last time chatting happily about our forthcoming journey home and Allie and Sarah deciding what they were going to do that afternoon. Not only had we received the good news about Sarah's health, but in contrast to that first depressing appointment, we had been reminded how different everything now felt.

There was another significant appointment during the first few weeks of Sarah's life: her existence had to be registered.

A friend of mine had worked temporarily in the Office of Registration of Births, Deaths and Marriages in South London. The Registry was run by a harridan of a woman, so completely insensitive and impervious to people's situations that her usual welcome when a member of the public approached the reception desk was barely to look up from her newspaper and to bark the curt questions, 'What are you here for? Birth, death or marriage?'

This opening query didn't seem to change no matter what state of emotion the person on the other side of the desk was in. A woman dressed head to toe in black, sobbing uncontrollably, a nervously coy young couple, or a mother proudly clutching her newborn infant would all be questioned in the same bored, disinterested tone. Service with a sneer.

There was, however, very little humour to be derived from our trip to register Sarah's birth. We were so ambivalent we had just not wanted to face this task, which is normally one of pride and pleasure. It was not because we were unsure of a name. She was Sarah from the day she was born. It was also becoming easier to venture into the outside world. It was just somehow that this symbolic act of the baby becoming a 'real' person in society didn't seem appropriate. It was as if this act of registration would take on a separate process in our situation with different rules and with a different significance attached.

We finally took Sarah to be registered on the day before the last legal day. We looked at the birth certificate and felt sad. Sarah Kate Merriman – a lovely name – but who was this Sarah Kate? If only we could peel away her Down's syndrome and behold the other Sarah Kate – our longed for daughter.

At that time, we were also beginning to have contact with a number of professionals – mainly from health departments. In addition to regular visits from the midwife, health visitor, GP and at least two physiotherapists, Allie also had to take Sarah for appointments with the speech therapist, hospital consultants and the community paediatrician. There were constant comings and goings and Sarah seemed to be an endless source of attention from all sorts of agencies and interested parties. We didn't think that we would have enough time for ourselves or Daniel ever again.

Allie also had to take Sarah to the local Child Development Unit for contact with various therapists. It was in a backwater of a hospital and was drab and dreary and she resented being funnelled into this depressing atmosphere. The only highlight was a larger than life Specialist Health Visitor, who, apart from being the voice of reason and hope, gave us very practical suggestions and exercises for encouraging Sarah's hypotonia (floppy muscles), her tongue control and general areas of stimulation. Although this was all extra work, at least we began to feel less helpless and could focus our energy on specific tasks.

Sarah had breastfed well from the moment of birth which was unusual for babies with Down's syndrome. However, she became rather unsettled in the evenings and the specialist health visitor felt that, because Allie was under stress, she wasn't producing enough milk. Sarah needed an additional feed and she thus suggested a milk supplement. Unfortunately Sarah refused to take a bottle no matter how much she was coaxed and cajoled. She screamed every time the bottle was placed anywhere near her and became more and more distressed. This of course disturbed us – not only because Sarah was upset, but also because it meant that she would be unhappy for several hours before she went to sleep. Like everything else at this time, we were convinced that this problem was only present because Sarah had Down's syndrome – it was just another manifestation of the diagnosis and thus more difficult to address.

Eventually we contacted the paediatric speech therapist in a desperate state and she was kind enough to visit us at home with a most impressive array of receptacles and containers, sporting every possible 'sucking' attachment. It was the nearest I've ever been to a Tupperware party and probably just as depressing.

Every type of vessel and mouthpiece was tried over a period of weeks and we must have spent hours and hours trying to get Sarah to have a little extra nutrition in this way. We both became desperately irritated by this palaver and by Sarah's reluctance to feed. It dawned on me that this was just the beginning of all the extra physical and emotional demands that Sarah was going to place on us for the rest of our lives.

Difficulty in feeding is not a problem that fortunately I have ever suffered. Even at my most miserable, I have not lost my appetite and have been able to eat well. Thus, on Valentine's Day, when Sarah was five weeks old, Allie and I went to the Czech club in North London to celebrate together. The Czech club is a venue that John, Allie's father, has frequented throughout all his London life. It's a lively and yet peculiarly intimate club, originally for Czech nationals, in a house in a residential street in North London. The restaurant has a small number of tables and is based in two rooms so that I always feel that I'm dining at a friend's house. This feeling is further enhanced by the fact that there is much more interaction between the various diners than in most restaurants. As soon as you enter the main dining area, the diners immediately look up from their Svíčková or Schnitzel and proceed to stare at you – long and hard. There is no pretence at trying to catch a surreptitious glance. They want to know who you are and why you are there. They then proceed to discuss you with their fellow guests and if you're lucky enough to have a Czech connection it may well be that a plate of dumplings will be despatched to your table with the compliments of a visiting professor from Prague.

This was the first time Allie and I had been out alone together since Sarah's birth. We wanted to have an evening away from the stresses and strains of our life and I had naively hoped we could enjoy a relaxed evening together. A temporary if superficial respite from the constant drama. It didn't turn out that way. Allie became preoccupied with the thought that Sarah would never have a Valentine's Day partner to celebrate with. Allie just couldn't allow herself to enjoy the evening as she was convinced that a similar experience would always be denied Sarah. She would always be deprived of evenings such as this and so how could Allie allow herself this pleasure?

Allie was sad and quiet all evening and when we got home she sobbed uncontrollably for what was about an hour in my arms. This was the first time that she had let herself lose control so freely since Sarah's birth. She was crying for the 'fantasy' child that had disappeared and for the dependent baby who had replaced it. This baby needed more love than most children and yet Allie did not yet feel this love. I was soon crying as well. We cried for the family we now were and for the one we should have been. We cried for our daughter whose life would be so different to our own and with whom we couldn't identify. We cried for the uncertainty of the future and most of all we cried for the unfairness of it all.

8. This Happy Breed of Men

Each culture, creed, race is plagued by stereotypical views of its behaviour. These identified 'traits' are the basis of discrimination and the effects of ageism, racism and sexism are all still rife in a society that remains basically conservative. People with mental illness and learning disability are no exception and those with Down's syndrome are particularly prone to uniform, but uninformed opinion. They do, in fact, tend to be the subject of trite observations in a way that would be considered abusive if they were being attributed on a racial basis. The notion that all Asians are shopkeepers, that the Chinese are only known for running restaurants and that black people are only gifted in music or sport is obviously untrue and yet the myths continue. One of the least obviously offensive, but extraordinarily patronizing descriptions of Afro-Caribbeans in the 1960s and 1970s as 'happy laughing people, who love music' is clearly unacceptable and it is also still unacceptable to describe people with Down's syndrome in this way.

Adults or children with Down's syndrome are not necessarily either 'happy and affectionate' or 'stubborn and difficult to control'. There may be a number of people with Down's syndrome who are mainly happy and affectionate and there may be a number who are also difficult and aggressive. Believe it or not, there may be some who are affectionate and aggressive! It may be true to say that some people with Down's syndrome are less socially inhibited and their emotions and frustrations are closer to the surface, but this does not imbue them with particular traits.

They don't all have particular talents such as music or mimicry or the sense of fun noted by Langdon Down, who in his series of papers published in 1866, 'Observations on an Ethnic Classi-fication of Idiots', wrote, 'They have considerable power of imitation, even bordering on mimics. They are humorous, and a lively sense of the ridiculous often colours their mimicry.'

There aren't characteristic behaviours linked to Down's syn-drome, but it is not easy to dispel these stereotypes once people are predisposed to recognize them. We only see what we have been advised to look for. It can be unsettling and alarming if we are surprised by the unexpected behaviour of a disabled person, who is supposed to act in a certain way.

There is in fact a great variety of character and personality within this particular population and they possess a multi-dimensional range of emotions and attitudes. Perhaps it is easier for us to accept these different types if we can sort and label them into neat parcels. Herman Hesse said, 'Nothing makes the multitude angrier than when someone forces them to change their opinion of him.' It is vital that we endeavour to change the existing view of people with Down's syndrome.

According to Cliff Cunningham, studies of children with Down's syndrome do not show evidence of a pre-described set of characteristics and in fact the behaviour of a child with Down's syndrome is similar to that of other children at the same level of development.

Of course, the behavioural aspect is not the only area where myths abound; Down's syndrome babies are not just born to older women. Three quarters of children with Down's syndrome are born to mothers under the age of thirty-five. Not every adolescent with Down's syndrome will exhibit behavioural prob-lems and not all the adults have a 'special gift'.

People with learning disabilities are stigmatized in many differ-ent ways and no more so than by Intelligence Quotient testing. This method of measuring intelligence has far-reaching effects on the lives of those with Down's syndrome and indeed their families.

In Michael Berube's book, *Life As We Know It*, he describes an Associated Press news story concerning a sixteen-year-old American high school footballer, Luke Zimmerman, who was acknowledged as 'a leader and an inspiration to his team-mates'. Luke has Down's syndrome and the story was supposed to show what can be achieved by some young men in his situation. Unfortunately, later in the piece, it states, 'Down Syndrome [U.S. terminology] children usually never develop beyond age eight, mentally.' It is this sort of misinformation that labels people with Down's syndrome and typifies the sort of generalizations that they have to suffer.

An average IQ score is about one hundred and anyone with a score of less than about seventy or seventy-five is considered to have a learning disability. The scores of people with Down's syndrome range from about twenty to one hundred and it is interesting to note that now there is a much greater expectation of achievement and thus more educational opportunities. The average IQ of a person with Down's syndrome has doubled since the Second World War.

An IQ score shows how quickly or slowly a child has developed compared with children of a similar age and does not take into account the fact that someone's mental ability might be the result of a language problem or a hearing or visual difficulty. Equally, the child's development is dependent on many aspects – educational opportunities, the home environment, family pressures and experiences and cultural expectations. It does not measure practical skills, social abilities or emotional maturity.

Even at the age of five, Sarah exhibits a sensitivity and an empathetic nature that would confound most other children of her age. She is always the first to greet me at the door when I return from work and ask if I had a 'good day' or a 'nice time' and if one of the family is upset or unwell, she is invariably the one to notice and remember and try to make things better. She judges our moods imperceptibly and seems to have an uncanny knack of knowing when something isn't quite right.

This level of 'sense and sensibility' cannot be measured and of course plays no part in the totting up process of points in testing 'intelligence'. The level of achievement is thus judged in conventional terms – an aptitude test, which undervalues personal skills. Intelligence comes in many guises and cannot merely be reduced to such methodology.

This social prejudice is also based on the visual image of Down's syndrome, which remains somewhat negative. The overweight, lethargic, bespectacled adult is still the picture that first comes to mind. Medical reasons such as thyroid dysfunction, which is more common in people with Down's syndrome, can often be a cause, but this is generally not known by the general public, who understandably link the syndrome with physical sluggishness. Despite the amount of information put out by the Down's Syndrome Association and Mencap, there remains much ignorance and unease among the general public. Until a positive image is encouraged and publicized in all aspects of our society and the general view altered, it is likely that the public's perception will continue to be somewhat ill-informed and often patronizing.

Children and adults with Down's syndrome need to be accepted in all areas of everyday life and they must be seen to be part of society – not outside it. Advertising plays an important part in creating trends by portraying normal, family life and yet, to my knowledge, apart from the odd charitable organization, a Mothercare catalogue from nearly ten years ago, and a very recent Benetton advertisement I have never seen a child or person with Down's syndrome encouraging the sale of a particular product on television or in a magazine. Is this because the image is too negative? Would the appearance of a child with learning disabilities really turn people off from buying clothes, breakfast cereals or toys? I can't believe the sight of a gleeful Sarah modelling her new dress or devouring her favourite ice cream would have a negative marketing effect. Families with children with Down's syndrome also lead very normal lives. We brush our teeth, play games and go on holidays and it is important that this normality is realized.

Despite all this, it is difficult to be critical of certain comments when you know that there is no malevolent intent and that people are merely trying to be sympathetic. The things people say are often meant well, but do sometimes have the opposite effect.

We tried to address some of the stereotypical views in one scene of *Minor Adjustment*. Amy has been admitted to hospital after a severe attack of croup. Her mother, Sarah, has stayed the night with her and it is now the following morning.

A hospital paediatric ward. Amy is playing in the background.

Woman: So, what's the matter with your child?

Sarah: Oh, Amy's got croup. She only came in yesterday, but she's much better – I'm hoping we can go home today.

Woman: Oh that's good.

Sarah: I didn't get much sleep last night.

Woman: Oh I know – it is difficult, isn't it? And some of the night staff are a bit noisy.

Sarah: Well, I suppose they have work to do.

Woman: Yes. True. Has your daughter been in hospital before?

Sarah: A couple of times.

Woman: Oh dear. Poor thing. I suppose they're not very healthy.

Sarah: *They?*

Woman: Down's syndrome children.

Sarah: Oh.

Woman: I couldn't help but notice. Although she is very pretty.

Sarah: For one of *them*, you mean.

Woman: Oh, I'm sorry, I didn't mean to offend you.

Sarah: It's all right.

Woman:	I hope you don't mind me asking, but did you know that she had Down's when you were pregnant?
Sarah:	No, I didn't.
Woman:	And you didn't have a test for it?
Sarah:	There was no reason to.
Woman:	Oh, I had all the tests with both my children. If anything had been wrong, I don't know what I would have done. I just couldn't possibly cope with a handicapped child.
Sarah:	Not everyone can. I'm certainly not saying every home should have one.
Woman:	Did you consider having her adopted?
Sarah:	No, not for a moment. Did you ever consider having your children adopted?
Woman:	No, of course not.
Sarah:	Then why do you ask me?
Woman:	Well, because … because she'll be dependent on you for the rest of your life.
Sarah:	And your children won't be?
Woman:	I just think it's a bit different. I mean isn't it unlikely that your daughter will ever have a job … or get married or … have children of her own?
Sarah:	And you're sure that both your children will have all those things. Aren't you lucky?
Woman:	I suppose you've got some compensations. After all, they are meant to be very affectionate and happy children.
Sarah:	Actually, Amy is both those things, but we like to think that's because she's Amy – not because she has Down's syndrome.
Woman:	No … no … of course not. But there are certain traits, aren't there? I mean, aren't they supposed to love music and dancing?
Sarah:	Yes – we're hoping she's going to be in the re-make of *South Pacific*.
Woman:	[pause] Actually, in a way, my daughter also has special needs.

Sarah:	Oh really?
Woman:	Oh, yes. Charlotte is extremely bright. She's been described as 'gifted'. Her school really don't stretch her sufficiently and we're having to get extra help. Of course, she is very advanced for her age.
Sarah:	Why is she in hospital?
Woman:	She fell out of a window and broke her leg.
Sarah:	[to herself] So, she's not that bright then. [Then, louder] Well, I hope she's back on her feet again … and back to school.
Woman:	Oh that's all right. I've brought her in some work. I wouldn't want her to miss out.
Sarah:	No, that would be terrible for you.
Woman:	How old is Amy?
Sarah:	Three … nearly four.
Woman:	I know this might sound awful, but what sort of mental age is she likely to have when she's an adult?
Sarah:	I beg your pardon.
Woman:	Well, have the experts made any predictions about what she's going to achieve?
Sarah:	No, they haven't, but she's doing very well – at her own pace.
Woman:	I'm sure she'll make some contribution. I've heard of one, who even worked in an old people's home. Everybody loved her.
Sarah:	Amazing, isn't it?
Woman:	Oh, there's Dr Thompson. I must have a word with her. You'll have to excuse me … [Going off and calling] Dr Thompson … could I just have …
Sarah:	… Stupid bloody woman. No wonder that girl fell out of a window – probably trying to run away from home. [Sighs deeply] Oh, I don't know … sometimes this is all too much. Come here, Amy. Mummy needs a hug.
Amy:	Mummy. Mummy.

Sarah: [tearful] Oh Amy ... I do love you...

Nurse: [approaching] Are you okay, Mrs Stubbs?

Sarah: Yes ... yes ... thank you ... Sister ... I'm all right.

Nurse: You know, there's really no need to worry about Amy, she's much better.

Sarah: Oh, it's not Amy that I'm upset about. It's the people around her that worry me.

Fade down

9. Further Reflections

The most difficult time during those first few months following Sarah's birth was first thing in the morning. I would feel bleak and hopeless on waking and wondered how I would survive the day – let alone the rest of my life. I remember asking a psychotherapist friend of ours whether it was common when depressed to feel significantly worse when one first wakes up and he responded wittily that I should read Freud's paper, 'Mourning and Melancholia'.

This intense deep sadness made me feel the urge to sleep in order to escape the real world. I remember having had the reverse feeling on finding myself awake after a nightmare and being delighted at what was the reality. Now my reality had become a nightmare from which I wanted to flee and my only method of achieving this was to sleep.

Fortunately Sarah slept through the night from day one. It was as if she knew that to exist within our family she would have to keep a low profile in those early weeks. I do wonder how I would have coped if I had been faced with the further exhaustion of broken nights during those weeks of turmoil.

The day's pattern seemed set. As the day wore on, life would take over and my spirits would lift. I clearly remember feeling almost jovial some evenings when friends and family gathered. At these times I would convince myself that my constant companion of dread was beginning to relinquish its grip . . . only to swallow me up again the following morning.

During the day my mind was in constant motion, my awareness was heightened to such a degree as to be intolerable at times.

My mind was in overdrive, everything seemed altered. Even ordinary familiar things – the view from our bedroom window – appeared different. Because of this, when I looked out, I expected the players in the scene to perform in some other way. How could the man across the road still clean his car so obsessively and so regularly? Was he not aware that the world had changed so significantly and was now a different place for us? I loathed his lack of insight into our situation which I would have thought would have given him different priorities. Of course I soon realized that this was incredibly self-indulgent and arrogant. My life had changed for ever, but why should his?

Who was he to know or care?

The love and care that was bestowed upon us during this period went a very long way in countering the feelings of despair. The phone became a drug at times. I needed a regular fix of support and any opportunity to make sense of what was happening by way of some enlightening words that would ease my burden.

At the same time this telephonic dependence also became intrusive and exposing. I would be forced to explain again how we were managing. The words became repetitive; an empty, rehearsed mantra that seemed to distance myself from the caller.

We also made regular trips to the hospital where Sarah was born to see Dr Mackinnon, the consultant paediatrician. She was tremendously helpful, but I do remember thinking that although Dr Mackinnon was marvellous, she couldn't change the fact that Sarah had Down's syndrome. What really was the point of seeing her? What was the point of anything anymore?

This question was answered in part when I met a young child with Down's syndrome soon after Sarah's birth. Jessica was then a year old and the energetic grapevine had put us together. Her mother, Bernice, was a friend of a friend and I had already been made aware of Jessica's existence at the time of her birth. I had even discussed with this mutual friend how I would never be able to cope if this happened to me and how the prospect was so awful, it didn't bear thinking about.

Now here I was waiting to meet Bernice and Jessica and feeling fearful of how I would react to this little girl, who was a stranger but to whom my own daughter was so fundamentally linked. I will never forget the broad smiles that greeted me as I opened the door. I almost forgot the purpose of their visit as the small child actively explored her surroundings, whilst her mother and I chatted animatedly. Jessica was inquisitive about the toys, about Sarah, and about everything around her.

Bernice was not the harassed and depressed person I had envisaged – quite the opposite. I was beginning to feel seeds of encouragement and hope as I talked to her and observed and played with her delightful child. My fears seemed to fall away.

Bernice did not deny her own shock and pain a year earlier, when her first, longed for child was born. However, experiencing them as they were now and simply seeing that they had survived was comfort indeed. Things that Bernice told me at that time have remained indelible in my mind.

The first was how at the beginning she had found it impossible to imagine waking up in the morning without 'Down's syndrome' rushing like a whirlwind into her consciousness. Now it seemed this was no longer the case. I remember feeling wholly doubtful this process would pass for me as long as I would live.

The second vivid memory was of how Bernice spoke of her pregnancy; she had eaten healthily, refused alcohol and practised yoga. She was a midwife's dream! The irony was that something pretty drastic had occurred at the moment of conception that all her good efforts couldn't change.

I had done much the same thing and had tried everything in my power to create a healthy environment for my unborn child. I had even taken things to the extreme and made up rules such as not standing in front of the microwave oven.

I realized I was being neurotic about it and we joked about

this. Andy said that instead of making sure I wasn't anywhere near the oven, I should actually climb inside the microwave so that the normal nine months pregnancy would only take four days!

I remember combining the joint experiences of our textbook approaches to the pregnancies and linking this to what I had read in a book about Down's syndrome by Mark Selikowitz. 'The presence of an additional chromosome adversely affects foetal survival; eighty percent of such pregnancies end in miscarriage. Children who are born with the syndrome may therefore be regarded as testimony to their mother's ability to support them during pregnancy despite this disadvantage.'

Could it be that the painstaking care we had both taken in our pregnancies had contributed to what could be considered as a far from healthy outcome?

I also remember a seminal conversation with Bernice's husband Ian on the telephone. I was bravely saying that at least we wouldn't have to worry about the evils of 'sex, drugs, rock and roll' as our daughters moved through adolescence. He quickly told me that he would not deny his daughter the prospect of experiencing these. He stopped me in my tracks. I had learned another new lesson. I began to look forward to future contact with this family. As a unit they had given me a massive boost to my level of adjustment and feeling of well-being. I needed to remain in touch.

A further early meeting with a young child with Down's syndrome was at a visit to a cranial osteopath – one of the many resources that I was advised could possibly enhance Sarah's future state of health.

I sat in the waiting room with Sarah in my arms and began to look around. I saw another mother holding a baby of about the same age. I looked at this baby and wondered if she also had Down's syndrome. Ridiculous, I told myself, I was beginning to suspect the syndrome in almost every other baby. My perspective was so altered by our own preoccupying experiences that I was becoming unable to separate it from anything around me. Before I could explore further what I decided must be yet another area of my developing madness, the mother began to talk to me.

'How old is your baby?'

'Four months,' I replied. And with my usual pre-emptive haste, I continued, 'She's got Down's syndrome.'

'So *is* mine and so *has* mine!' came her reply.

It turned out her little girl was just six days older than Sarah. This contact proved of tremendous importance as this family were Jewish and introduced me to a therapeutic playgroup run by Norwood Child Care, a North London social services organization for Jewish families.

This playgroup at Norwood's Family Centre gave parents of young children with a variety of newly diagnosed special needs an opportunity to talk together with a facilitator while their children enjoyed various play activities. This play was supervised by child development workers who had skills and experience in stimulating specific areas of development and were supported by a team of volunteers. These workers also made weekly home visits to do individual developmental programmes with the children, similar to the Portage programmes. I was able to talk about my feelings unhindered as Daniel and Sarah were either busy thrashing about in a 'ballpond' or were held spellbound in the Sensory Room which was full of lights, sounds, movement and tactile objects. They were also given the opportunity to play with ordinary equipment and toys and they both always enjoyed their visits to the centre.

This weekly group became a lifeline for me and I would long for Thursday mornings. This became my refuge, the one place I could go where I could feel like other parents. We were not going to be singled out as different, we weren't on show, we didn't need to explain to each other why we were there – the mutual understanding was palpable.

Strangely, this unexpected turn in my life had propelled me towards a somewhat neglected area of my world, but one for which I had struggled to find a forum. The fact that I was Jewish was central to my life – it was a vital part of my identity and yet I could not explain what being Jewish was. For me, it didn't involve a religious side, a community aspect or even a cultural component.

The fact of the Holocaust and its very direct effect on both my parents and their extended families has been, I'm sure, what has made me so conscious of my Jewish background.

During my first pregnancy, I pondered about how I was going to pass on this somewhat nebulous Judaism to the next generation, especially as Andy isn't Jewish. In Judiastic law, the Jewish line passes through the mother, but what did this really mean?

I did attend a mixed faith playgroup at a synagogue at the time, but then I'm afraid I became rather apathetic and the pressures of motherhood and work supplanted my good intentions. Andy suggested that the best way of introducing Daniel to the faith was to do what we had always done: eat bagels for breakfast, go to White Hart Lane regularly and watch as many episodes of Bilko as possible.

Sarah's arrival had given me a definite focus for a Jewish upbringing for my children, which was going to be part of our everyday life. Not only was Norwood at that time to become a resource to help us with Sarah and our needs as a family with a disabled daughter, but also as a source of cultural and religious significance. Various festivals were celebrated in a lively, warm atmosphere and we began to understand a little more about our roots.

The days passed and I felt a sense of achievement for surviving another day, another week or another month. I had a strong instinct that if only time would pass quickly, everything would gradually feel easier. I wished time away and rejoiced as I turned another page of the calendar. I fantasized Sarah as an eight-year-old and for some reason – perhaps thinking of Lily in the United States – began to feel excited about this prospect. My future image of myself with Sarah was of a mother on an even keel coping and content with a daughter with a complete and beautiful persona.

Amongst the huge correspondence that we seemed to be receiving during this period were two letters that appeared to be circulars and so were not opened with the usual enthusiasm until later in the day. I opened the first and a leaflet featuring a photograph of a middle-aged woman with very obvious Down's syndrome features fell on my lap. The face looked up at me with childlike glee and in very simple writing underneath this woman described the farm community she belonged to, stating that they required more funds. I was not prepared for this. I was not yet ready to contemplate Sarah's long-term future – after all she had barely been born. I felt angry and irrationally felt someone was attempting to torture me. I had been unfairly targeted.

I angrily opened the second letter . . . I had won first prize in the Trade Union lottery – a significant amount that I should have been grateful for at the time. Instead of being pleased at this good fortune, I felt unsettled because I had never won anything in this way and I wondered why I had been singled out so mysteriously. The pleasure of winning money was superseded by a feeling of victimization. Ordinary situations were taking on new rules and resonances and I no longer felt in control of my responses to things.

I had lost all my points of reference.

My overriding preoccupation was why had this happened to me? At the time I thought that Sarah had Down's syndrome because I had wanted a girl too much and this was somehow my punishment. I should have just believed the miracle of having a child was enough and focused on my wish for a healthy one rather than on its gender.

However, I believe it did help that Sarah was a girl. I had my ideal family: an older boy and a younger girl. This ideal stemmed partly from my own childhood wish for an older brother and was perhaps exacerbated by images in the media.

For some reason it was very important for me to dress Sarah in pink or at least in girls' clothes. I had planned to put the second baby in Daniel's old clothes whatever its sex – partly for practical reasons and partly because I had liked a tomboy image. I think what happened was that having had a label slapped on her from birth, I didn't want her individuality compromised in any other way. There could also have been an element of desire to highlight the only aspect I felt proud of at that stage – that she was a girl. Irritatingly, this idyll of older boy, younger girl still persists. When I hear of a girl born after a first-born son I experience a pang of jealousy which remains confused with the fact that I too have this pattern of offspring.

I began to think more philosophically about it and I spent a lot of time desperately trying to discover a reason for why this had happened to us. I think that when there is no objective answer, the mind can search out and pinpoint almost anything. I decided that perhaps the circumstances that had caused us to conceive a child with Down's syndrome were predestined as part of a master plan and that it was all beyond our control.

I had for a long time been aware that something would need to happen to me to jolt me out of my lucky and privileged existence. Alongside this, however, had been the contradictory feeling of 'it won't happen to me'.

I remember when Sarah was about two months old I was sitting with two of my dearest friends who had both faced very difficult circumstances in their twenties. One had been seriously injured in a car crash and the other had been stricken with cancer. Strangely, I understood that if I was to be tested, it would not be in the same ways as my friends. My challenge was to be the mother of a disabled child. This task would demand everything I thought I was good at. But, what it now exposed to me was that I was not the warm, capable person I would have myself believe. I was a fraud.

I could not even love my own sweet baby daughter who was actually a joy to care for. She fed and slept well and was soon to be smiling her beautiful smile. At other moments, rather than thinking I now knew the nature of the cross I was to bear, I felt that as this unexpected thing had happened to me, so would everything else. The floodgates to potential disasters had been opened wide. I was no longer immune. I found it hard to face the outside world of babies and children, but for the benefit of all of us, I knew I had to make the effort. I eventually dragged myself to a mother and toddler group when Sarah was about three months old. This particular group unsurprisingly seemed to be totally centred on pregnancy, birth, babies and pre-school children. Discussions seemed to involve very little else. I suspected Sarah and I were objects of morbid interest. We were their worst nightmare – objects of pity.

This was perhaps purely my own perception borne out of intense envy of other mothers whose children were 'perfect'. I resented what seemed to be mindless moans about feeding difficulties, sleeping problems, feelings of isolation – all the things I had enjoyed talking about following Daniel's birth. At that time, comparing notes on baby minutiae had been my major preoccupation. I remember one woman whinging about what seemed to me a most insignificant setback in her birth plan. I had to bite back my words, 'Well, you had your perfect daughter at the end of it, so just be grateful for that.'

I did find this playgroup experience very difficult at the beginning. It highlighted the differences in our situations and illuminated my vulnerabilities and dark side. However, after some weeks, I actually started to relax and even started to enjoy myself. Once we had gone beyond obsessing about baby care, I realized there were some very stimulating women in the group with a multitude of other interests and backgrounds. I was reminded of other worlds and existences and through this I rediscovered myself. I had taken such a confidence knock as a mother that I had lost sight of my abilities. Through my involvement with some of these people I felt affirmed.

As well as this unexpected outcome for myself, Daniel needed to be given every chance to mix with friends of his own age. I like to believe my parenting of Daniel did not suffer to any great degree at this time of turmoil. On many occasions he lifted my gloom and I appreciated him more than ever.

It must have been very hard for Daniel in those early weeks. I would sometimes be unable to stop myself crying in front of him. I was aware of how children believe the reactions of their parents come about because of something they themselves have done or who they are. I was very keen to dispel any feelings of this kind should they have existed. I explained that my feeling sad was nothing at all to do with him and that I was sad because it would take Sarah longer than other children to learn things. I told Daniel Sarah had Down's syndrome, as I wanted these words to feel familiar. Words that could be expressed honestly and even perhaps one day . . . proudly.

My feelings for Sarah during those first few months very slowly began to change. Mere duty turned into feelings of protectiveness, which in turn reflected flickerings of wary love. However, I remained almost continually aware of her diagnosis. I felt ashamed that any loving feelings were still so tentative, inconsistent and dispersed. I had always imagined that whoever my child was, whatever and whoever they would become, I would love them unconditionally. This was not now the case. There was a condition. Normality. This was my requirement and I hated my deluded self. Sarah was healthy and objectively a delight to mother. Sarah made perfect sense. It was me. I was the one who couldn't make sense of Sarah.

10. Thursday's Child has Far to Go

Two middle-aged Jewish women are sitting on a park bench.
   'Oy . . . Oy . . . Oy!' says one of the women. The other shrugs her shoulders and nods knowingly. The first shakes her head and utters a 'Teh!' The second raises her eyebrows and lifts both hands up in a gesture of hopelessness. The first woman lets out a low moan and places her head in her hands.
   After a short silence, the second woman turns to the first, looks her straight in the eye and says, 'Listen, I thought we weren't going to talk about the children.'

Worries about our children are all consuming. The cot's too small – he's got no room to play; it's too big – he'll grow up an agoraphobic. He's not warm enough – he'll get hypothermia; he's too hot – he'll dehydrate. We worry that they're too pale or that they've been in the sun too much. They don't get enough fresh air – always reading; they spend too much time outside and not enough time learning to play the piano. Why doesn't he ever ride that bicycle we bought him?; oh no, he's much too young to go on the road. They're too lazy; they're working too hard – they need a break. They're naughty; they're goody-goodies. They can't take care of themselves; they're bullies. They're too dependent on us; they've grown up too quickly and don't need us anymore.
   The anxieties are endless. Parents are forever in a state of self-doubt about how they are performing and if they are really doing the very best for their children. The health and happiness of the children is paramount. When you have a child with Down's

syndrome, you experience the ordinary concerns, but with the extra worry that your child is even more vulnerable than most. It is your responsibility to safeguard without overprotecting.

Allie and I have often discussed whether it is easier to know from birth that one's child has a disability or whether one can face the situation with greater security if you discover that there is a problem when you have already formed an attachment with your child. Knowing within an hour of her birth that Sarah had a disability certainly made it much more difficult to feel immediate love for her, but at least on a practical level we knew – from an extremely early stage of her existence – that she was going to need a lot more help than Daniel. Everything from feeding to toilet training, from talking to walking was going to take longer with Sarah and we would have to be patient. The quote that came to mind was one by H. G. Wells: 'Adapt or perish, now as ever, is nature's inexorable imperative.'

It's strange that, looking back, there wasn't one professional during the first year that would commit herself to the fact that Sarah would walk or talk. The uncertainty about her speech seemed more understandable, but I still have not come across a child or adult with Down's syndrome who could not walk. We were advised, however, that there were three vital things that Sarah must have in her first year. Stimulation, stimulation and stimulation. Thus no stone was left unturned in efforts to produce a response from Sarah.

Mobiles (we had more than a trailer park) were hung from every possible place, toys were poked and rattled in Sarah's face with monotonous regularity and we constantly engaged in babbling and gurgling, pulling faces, singing songs, clicking fingers, and clapping hands. We gave her objects to bang together, different textures to touch and feel, we stroked her fingers to help improve manipulation, we massaged her to help tone up the muscles. Poor Sarah was probably desperate for some peace and quiet, but by God she wasn't going to get it when we were around. No possible motivational moment could be lost. This girl's full potential would not be left to chance. She must be stimulated to within an inch of her life!

We endeavoured to ascertain that her hearing was normal (hearing problems are quite common with Down's syndrome) by producing a cacophony of sounds from a large number of instruments and contraptions at different distances and angles. To encourage the tracking of her eyes, we wagged forefingers in front of her like a couple of deranged cricket umpires.

Although I played my part as much as possible, Allie was more involved in giving Sarah every opportunity to learn and develop and like most parents of a child with Down's syndrome, she soon became quite an expert. Numerous books, papers and articles were read and digested and friends and family never wasted an opportunity to send us relevant material from any number of sources.

The future goal was independence in whatever shape or form and in whatever context Sarah could cope – but in order to achieve that independence, Sarah had to be dependent on lots of people.

One of our most stalwart professionals during that time was Carol Phillips, the specialist health visitor. Employed by the local health authority, Carol was experienced, empathetic and efficient with immense energy, which she devoted to her work. She visited regularly and was always available at the end of a telephone in times of crisis. She was ruthless in her commitment and nothing was too much trouble. We learned a great deal from her and each month she gave us a new list of tasks for Sarah, which we felt duty-bound to have completed by the next time she called.

Sarah's gross motor development was delayed somewhat and Carol stressed the importance of exercises to help. Very soon after her birth we were rolling Sarah from side to side to strengthen her legs, holding her in a special way to build up her back muscles and balancing her on rolled up towels to learn about the saving reflexes of her arms. We were pinning her legs back to get her to kneel, pulling her arms behind her and forcing her to the floor on her tummy to raise her head. There were times when I expected her to beat the ground with the palms of her hands in an act of theatrical submission.

Carol used to end every 'work' list with the words, 'Sarah is doing well, but we need to keep up the momentum.' And so we did . . .

Sarah was thus subjected to an intensive course of occupational therapy and also had treatment from a cranial osteopath and a private physiotherapist. The local speech therapist made a number of domiciliary calls, which were of great benefit. Being in her own environment obviously helped Sarah, but this was not surprising because, as my father put it, 'Clarity begins at home.'

There were a number of special toys that we were told would help Sarah and so naturally these had to be purchased. Grandmothers were despatched to various London department stores with strict orders for the latest in remedial finger puppets, tactile activity kits and 'Koosh' balls, which could all help Sarah in our quest for a state of 'total activation'. If we had been on performance related pay as parents at that time, we would have been millionaires.

In July 1992, Susie Gaffin, our development worker from Norwood, began the Portage Early Education Programme with Sarah. Portage consists of lists of 624 behaviours which are divided into six areas of development: infant stimulation, self-help, motor, socialization, cognitive and language. The main aim of these lists is to assist in the design of teaching activities for the individual child in an extremely detailed way so that even the tiniest progression is noted and extended.

It was important to view Sarah's development in such a concrete way and to be given specific guidance on exactly how to help her. In this way, although we felt that her overall progress was painfully slow, we could see that she was actually attaining skills, however gradually. Natural responses and spontaneous play seemed to take second place as Sarah's every move and gesture was recorded. The science of child development was at work!

Susie was also enormously helpful as an emotional crutch for Allie. Although only in her mid-twenties, she somehow had what it took to offer really therapeutic support, as well as working on the tasks with Sarah. After several months, Susie left to go to Israel and she was replaced by a developmental worker from the local borough's Home Intervention Service, Sarah Loxton. Sarah continued the Portage work for many months and we were equally lucky that she was also an exceptional worker, who brought with her enormous care and commitment. Sarah finally left to travel around the world. I hope that it was merely coincidence that these women who had worked so closely with our family both felt the urge to escape to far-away shores!

Communication can come in many shapes and forms using body language, tone of voice and movement. Up until now, these forms of contact were really the only ways that we had been able to relate to Sarah on an intellectual basis. If Sarah was to be fully accepted, it would be easier if we could find a two-way process of communication. In that fashion, we could really understand her and get to know her in the same way as we had Daniel.

We were made aware that people with Down's syndrome have a more developed visual perception than auditory perception. Whilst still using the spoken word, the use of signs can ameliorate communication at an early stage. The Makaton method of 'signing' was introduced to us as the best method to help Sarah develop her speech and communication skills. Makaton was originally developed by a speech therapist, Margaret Walker, in the mid-1970s. It was then, however, used as an aid to communication with adults who had severe learning disabilities or were deaf and lived in institutions. Hence, stage one of the process enables the user to sign words such as 'nurse', 'doctor' and 'cigarette'. Obviously Sarah didn't need to know the sign for cigarette as her addiction at six months was in the form of rusks rather than nicotine.

Sarah soon learned a number of signs and developed her own gestures, which didn't need to be exactly prescribed as long as all the participants knew what they signified and they were used consistently. In fact we soon adapted some of the signs for our own benefit if we wanted to avoid a particular word in front of the children.

Daniel was particularly interested in this method of communication and like any other five-year-old was quick to learn and remember the various signs. His particular favourites were the signs for 'brother' (a thumbs up whilst rubbing his knuckles together), 'dog' (holding his hands like paws and moving them up and down in front of his chest), and 'sausage' (his own version of the sign, which appeared extremely rude).

Because Sarah adapted the Makaton signs that she could understand and perform, it gave her a way of communicating that was truly hers – a language that defined her as an individual – something that we had been finding it hard to do. My only concern had been that Makaton might actually prevent Sarah from speaking and that she might not bother to use a word where a sign might do. However, we were advised that we should always attempt to use the word in conjunction with the sign so that the two actions would be considered synonymous. Once the word had been learned and Sarah knew the meaning and could pronounce it correctly, the sign could be discarded. It is interesting that although Sarah now expresses herself verbally, she sometimes uses a favourite sign in conjunction or on the odd occasions when she cannot make herself understood or she forgets the word. We use Makaton less and less, but will occasionally employ a sign when a new concept is proving difficult.

We were aware that Sarah's communication difficulties might cause problems when planning for Sarah's care when Allie went back to work part-time. Daniel had been with the same child-minder, Annie Sabbagh, since he was two and we had hoped that Sarah would be able to do the same. We were eager for Sarah to be able to follow in Daniel's footsteps as it seemed imperative that her experience should be as 'normal' as possible. Sarah was likely to get much more stimulation from being with other children in a more formal environment than with a tired and emotionally drained middle-aged couple like us!

Of course, we could not now assume that Annie would have Sarah, who would, after all, need special attention and might demand more time and energy than the other children. Might other parents object that someone like Sarah would be mixing with their children?

We needn't have worried. Annie reminded us that on the day that Sarah was born, she had told us that there would be no question of her not caring for Sarah. Her offer had been lost in all the drama at the time, but we were now extremely grateful when we realized what a significant gesture this was at the time of Sarah's birth.

When Sarah went to Annie at the age of eleven months, her health, future development and capabilities were naturally an unknown quantity, but we were lucky that Annie's training as a nursing sister at Great Ormond Street Hospital for Children had brought her into contact with a lot of children with Down's syndrome. She had also worked at an institution for children with learning and physical disabilities in the 1970s and so was quite aware of any inherent problems.

Annie's philosophy was to accept Sarah as just another one of her charges. She maintains that all the children she looks after have their own quirks, interests and needs. 'Wait and see, but I'm sure she'll be fine,' were her comforting words.

Sarah actually settled in reasonably quickly and Annie, her staff and the other children were soon using Makaton signing, although Annie was keen not to make Sarah very different from the other children. She did, however, feel that Sarah required extra stimulation whilst at play and spent additional time trying to involve Sarah in some of the activities.

Sarah still goes to Annie's after school and in the school holidays and continues to enjoy the fun and homely atmosphere that exists in the house – not to mention the various day trips and outings. We are forever grateful for Annie's confidence and optimism about Sarah at a time when we found it difficult to feel these things.

As Sarah's first birthday approached, instead of excitedly thinking how we were going to celebrate, we dreaded the event. Neither of us wanted to admit it, but we really didn't want to have a party – enforced jollity is not very appealing at any time, but having to pretend to be happy on your child's birthday seemed desperately sad. After avoiding the subject for a while, we both revealed that we just couldn't bear to participate in all the rigmarole of jelly and ice cream, 'pass the parcel' and the usual 'Happy Birthday' refrains. She was only a year old, after all, and wouldn't know what was happening. We were certain that we would be able to face it next year – and who knows, maybe even enjoy it. Of course, we didn't want to deprive Sarah of some acknowledgement that this was indeed an important milestone and so we decided we would all go away for a couple of days.

We spent the weekend in a pub in Dunwich and managed to mark the occasion in calm and reflective mood. I've holidayed by the Suffolk coast since I was about ten and I've always held a special affection for that area. It's peaceful, unspoilt and has a gentle pace. I always remember a Southwold park keeper wearing a badge which read 'Don't ask me to hurry I'm from Suffolk'. It seemed the perfect place to be with Sarah on her first birthday.

I've always admired the matter of fact, down to earth attitude of the Suffolk people. Some years ago, an elderly man whom we knew very well was widowed and I went to see him, rather dreading the meeting and not knowing quite what to say. His wife of over fifty years had just died and I tried to be sympathetic, supportive, understand his loss and get him to talk about the pain that he must be going through. 'Oh no,' he said, 'you don't want to worry about me, I'll be all right and in any case I've gone out and bought myself a microwave!'

This stoical approach was further exemplified by a conversation with a woman in the pub on our weekend away. We explained we were there because of Sarah and she immediately confided in us. 'Oh yes,' she said, 'that is bad luck. Still, you can't let these things worry you. I've lost three children in accidents and cot deaths and what have you and I'm OK – you see, I've still got six left.'

Whilst therapists and counsellors might throw their hands up in horror at such denial and lack of insight, I was immediately attracted to this woman's philosophy. When I think of some of the self-obsessive minutiae and minor concerns that are discussed on analysts' couches – particularly in North London – I am always heartened by this direct approach to the more real and serious challenges to the human condition. In the nearby seaside village of Walberswick, I saw a man wearing a T-shirt with the slogan 'Just do it' emblazoned across the front. Perfect for the Suffolk approach, I thought. Life sponsored by Nike.

11. Milestones

The need for parents to document the accomplishments of their children is a natural process. With Daniel, we would delight in his first words, exalt his first few steps and proudly display his early artwork. Virtually every week of his life is documented on videofilm. By the arrival of the second child these events do not seem so remarkable and there is not nearly so much detail kept. Of course this was not true of Sarah because with her, every achievement was eagerly anticipated and marked. Her capabilities were a testament – not only to her determination to overcome her disabilities – but also to all the people who had helped us. Her achievements enabled us to feel that we were doing as much as we possibly could for her, something that every parent with a disabled child needs continual reassurance about.

Like Christopher Robin and Alice, Sarah also went down to the Palace, When Sarah was a little over a year old, Allie took her to an early learning group for disabled children and their siblings named PALACE (Play and Learn and Creative Education). PALACE had originated about three years previously through a special needs health visitor bringing together a group of local parents with various disabled pre-school children for coffee mornings.

The individuals within this group had found strength in one another and realizing how poorly resourced the area was in terms of creative outlets for their children, PALACE was born. An administrator, a 'conductive education' physiotherapist, an aromatherapist and a play organizer were employed. Young adults with learning disabilities provided voluntary help and all the services were provided free of charge.

Our health service physiotherapist seemed to have run out of ideas to help Sarah and did not appear to treat her as a priority. Allie was therefore delighted to discover this conductive education therapist bursting with enthusiasm about the various methods she could employ to stimulate Sarah's development at every level.

These initial weekly sessions did, however, take Sarah and Allie aback somewhat; a rather regimented routine was involved in a small group setting of children of similar age and with a variety of disabilities. Sarah was being pushed physically in ways that seemed premature. She screamed as she was forced to assume various positions, as her arms and legs were moved in rhythmically defined motions. Allie found Sarah's howls of discomfort very hard to bear and she became very uncertain about this programme.

She wondered if it might not be kinder and easier to stick to a more *laissez-faire* approach. Could Sarah's clear antipathy for these activities even be counterproductive as well as uncomfortable? Allie felt guilty. After all, our small child was communicating very vociferously that she was not ready for what she was being asked to do. Her cries were going unheard and yet there seemed very little evidence of the value of this approach. The only proof was the older children Allie had observed in another group who seemed to be enjoying and clearly benefiting from their sessions and who had also apparently loathed their earlier involvement. It was because of this that Allie continued to take Sarah to this pro-active therapy despite her reservations.

After some weeks, fortunately, Sarah quite suddenly ceased crying during the physical activities and slowly began to enjoy thoroughly the subsequent parts of the session, which were designed to employ children's everyday activities as a basis for learning. There was a fairly rigorous programme of repetitive 'action' songs, turn-taking games, 'potty sitting' and relaxation exercises. Sarah began to recognize her friends in the group and anticipate the next activity. She became impatient at times, having to wait her turn, but was always very generous when clapping her hands to congratulate her peers on their achievements (not to mention her own!). Following this session, she was covered in aromatic oils and massaged by the aromatherapist. This was relaxing as well as stimulating for her body. The type of oils changed according to Sarah's particular health needs.

Between these more formal activities at PALACE, Sarah played with their abundant supply of toys and equipment. As she got older, she was encouraged to paint, stick and make things with the attendant play organizer. She enjoyed the music and singing groups and made a number of friends.

While Sarah was occupied, Allie was also able to benefit from the mutual understanding and support from staff and other parents and from the monthly aromatherapy treatment offered to exhausted parents!

The centre has been a salient example of self-help and parent empowerment and proves that – even in the most unhealthy of political climates – parents really can strive for the specific needs of their children to create an environment that only grass roots know-how can achieve. I have faith that this is the way forward for groups of this kind and hope that in time, Sarah herself, along with her peers, will be fully involved and given the power to make decisions and choices about future resources.

During this period, we were always being asked if Sarah had learned to walk yet. It had become a major issue and one that was beginning to worry us. Despite all the intervention, state-of-the-art baby walkers and much encouragement, she seemed to be getting nowhere fast. Actually this isn't strictly true – she was getting somewhere fast, but by using her backside as a mode of transport.

We had become so tired of Sarah's bottom shuffling. Because

she had never crawled, it was, at first, a relief to know that she could transport herself quite speedily on her backside and then her somewhat idiosyncratic action was amusing. But by the age of two, we really felt she was ready to walk and became extremely frustrated at her inability to do so. We began to wonder if she would ever feel the need to get up on her pins. She certainly didn't seem that bothered, but we were becoming more so . . .

I couldn't wait for Sarah to be walking beside me, holding my hand. I didn't care in what manner she achieved this, however ungainly or slow. I just wanted to see her put one foot in front of the other! The symbolism connected to her walking became very strong as her first longed for steps came to represent her first strides towards independence. If these were to be achieved, we could then look with a new optimism at the road before us. Once she could walk, the contemplation of all other areas of delay would seem more manageable.

As a birthday present to her maternal grandfather, on 4 February 1994, Sarah finally walked unaided for the first time. It was still another two months before she could maintain any lasting motion and equilibrium, but the thrill of seeing her walk for the first time was breathtaking. The reward of each new stage is all the greater for all the investment involved. If Neil Armstrong thought he was taking a giant step for mankind with his first few steps on the moon, he should have seen our reaction when Sarah completed what we considered to be the terrestrial equivalent.

Sarah was beginning to do things for herself which showed that she had more than a basic understanding of the world around her. She watched how things were done and then copied them. She was gradually emerging from her chromosomal chrysalis into an individual with preferences, interests, and choices.

She started to enjoy 'action' songs and eventually when she did learn the words and actions to 'Row, Row, The Boat' and 'Wind The Bobbin Up' and repeated them with such regularity and volume, we almost regretted the great strides she had made in those early years!

Sarah loved watching a video of songs and rhymes with Makaton signs performed by the children's presenter Dave Benson Phillips who is extremely popular with all children and brings totally unbridled enthusiasm to his work. Sarah has enjoyed watching this video for two years now and she still asks for it regularly, joining in the words and signs with as much energy as Mr Benson Phillips.

Sarah had always liked books – she used to play with them even before she knew what they were for. Now she was beginning to look at them properly and particularly enjoyed the Spot series – carefully lifting each illustrated flap to see what was underneath. She obviously couldn't understand the words and wasn't able to describe much of what she saw, but she was taking an interest and more importantly choosing which books she wanted to view.

Looking back over these first two years my overriding memories are those involving the huge emphasis on stimulation and the close scrutiny of each aspect of Sarah's development. This may appear a rather impersonal and unspontaneous recollection of a precious time with one's child, but this is not the whole story. Through these various activities, the everyday care of Sarah and the passage of time, a subtle but vital change had occurred in our feelings towards her. Sarah was now a little girl in her own right – her diagnosis had become just one of the many facets of her being and Sarah herself had come to life.

Up until four years ago, when I heard the word 'milestones' I just thought of the great jazz composition by Miles Davis. I thought of the explosive drumming of Tony Williams, the driving bass lines of Ron Carter, the power of tenor saxophonist George Coleman and the lyrical piano of Herbie Hancock. Now, when I hear the word 'milestones' I think of the outstanding achievements of Sarah Merriman.

When Sarah was born, she was a Down's syndrome baby, who happened to be our daughter, and now as time passed, she had become our daughter, Sarah, who happened to have Down's syndrome.

12. Good Luck in the Studio

My father, Eric Merriman, was a legend in his own lunchtime . . . quite literally. He was the creator and writer of the popular radio show, *Beyond Our Ken*, which was broadcast in the 1950s and early 1960s on the BBC *Light Programme*, regularly drawing ten million listeners. The show starred Kenneth Horne, Kenneth Williams, Bill Pertwee, Betty Marsden and Hugh Paddick and during the height of its success, the audience would queue around the Paris Cinema in Lower Regent Street where the show was recorded at twelve-thirty every Wednesday. Although the tickets were free, the show had such a devoted following that they were in huge demand and it was rumoured (at least by my dad) that ticket touts used to loiter around the theatre selling at hugely inflated prices.

With the laughter still ringing in his ears, Dad would come home and start to write the next episode, which would have to be delivered to the producer by the following Monday. In all, he wrote over a hundred shows – somewhat different from the team approach now used in American situation comedy where anything up to ten writers can work on a single script.

The Paris was such a favourite studio of Dad's that he actually had it written into his contract that he would only record the show there. At the time, according to my father, the other BBC studios were cold and impersonal, but at the Paris there was an intimate contact between the audience and the performers.

The Paris Cinema, as its name implies, was originally a 'picture house' showing Continental films. It also happened to have been constructed deep underground. I'm not sure whether that's why it was considered suitable for *risqué* French films, but I do know that it became a godsend to the BBC when it was turned into a recording studio where wartime broadcasts could be transmitted from the heart of Piccadilly in the comparative safety of an underground shelter.

It was at the Paris that such famous comedy shows as *ITMA* (*It's That Man Again*) starring Tommy Handley and *Hi Gang* with London's favourite American residents, Ben Lyon and Bebe Daniels, were made. Both of these were sort of 'defiant' comedy shows – propaganda in a way – to prove that London could keep its sense of humour amid the incessant wartime bombing.

My father was then only in his teens, but already had a penchant for comedy. He thrived on those early radio shows, little knowing that one day he would be emulating the writers and artistes he so admired. In fact, Kevin Kavanagh, the son of Ted Kavanagh, *ITMA*'s scriptwriter, became Dad's agent for many years.

Fans of *Beyond Our Ken*, who followed every character and catchphrase with ecstatic laughter and applause, would leave messages and small gifts of appreciation on his seat in the front row.

Of course I am biased, but the writing was excellent and combined with such a terrific cast, the show became a comedy classic. I remember Dad telling me, however, that on one occasion he had become somewhat irked when one of the show's producers had, in a press interview, praised the cast to the hilt, but failed to mention the importance of the script and the skill of my dad's writing. The producer had actually said that the cast were so clever that they could make the telephone directory funny. At the read-through of the next show, instead of handing out scripts, Dad distributed telephone directories to the various cast members and said, 'OK . . . now make me laugh.' Unfortunately this rather backfired on him as Kenneth Williams – who else? – rose to the challenge and had everyone in hysterics by just reading a list of names and addresses in a series of different voices!

I have to say, however, in Dad's defence, that the writer is often the unsung hero of comedy and it is only in recent years that there has been any real recognition that sketches or sitcoms are not just made up on the spot by the performers. Actors and actresses in successful television productions are often household names, but with very few exceptions, the public does not know the identities of the writers of the shows.

In 1962, my father was at his office writing another episode of *Beyond Our Ken*, when he heard by telephone that my brother Christopher, aged eight months, had died. He and his agent rushed home to find my mother distraught. Christopher had been sleeping in his cot and my mother, who was on the telephone, suddenly ended her call feeling that something was wrong. She went into his bedroom, but he was already dead from what was termed later as a cot death.

I was only seven years old at the time but I remember the scenes very clearly. I also recall the following day being summoned to see the headmaster, desperately racking my brains to remember – and then find an excuse for – the heinous crime that I must have committed. I sat down in a huge leather chair in his study and was told, 'Some children are too good for this earth and God needs them in heaven.' I stumbled out of his study rather bemused at his words but grateful that he obviously didn't know what I had done wrong either.

Although I do not have a clear memory of specific incidents in the months after this event, I was aware of the desperately sad atmosphere in the house as my parents tried to come to terms with the shock of what had happened. They never referred to Christopher's death in front of me, but even at my young age I knew that they were suffering and were trying to shelter me from their unhappiness. I was really too young to suffer any real feelings of grief or loss myself and I do believe the only long-term effect on my own life was that my parents, quite under-standably, did tend to overprotect me for a number of years.

The death of one's child must be near unbearable to a parent in any circumstance, but the guilt that is associated with this sort of 'accident' remains with families for ever. There is always the feeling that, somehow, they could have done something to prevent the tragedy. My mother and father were no exception and for years felt responsible for Christopher's death. It was somewhat ironic that Allie and I would have very similar feelings when Sarah was born. Intellectually we knew we could not have prevented Sarah's diagnosis, but we did nevertheless feel guilty that we had produced a baby that was not perfect and who was sure to go on to lead a disastrous life. We also felt guilty about the possible implications of her arrival on her brother.

Another similarity in the situation between Sarah and Chris-topher was the insensitive remarks – albeit unknowingly – that were made to both Allie and me and to my parents. They were accused of being selfish because they didn't have more children and were told that it was unfair that I should be an only child.

There was very little discussion about Christopher for many years and it was only with Sarah's birth that they started to talk about it more openly. I remember thinking that perhaps the Merriman dynasty was not meant to have more than one child and that we should somehow have known not to have attempted to have more children. The link between Christopher's death and Sarah's birth seemed too much to bear as at the time both seemed to be tragic events in my life.

Despite being shocked and distraught, my father had to continue to finish the script that he had been working on. The old adage was true: 'The show must go on.' He couldn't, however, complete the sketch that he had been working on when he first heard the news and left it thinking that he could never return to it. A few weeks later, however, he decided to have another go at it and in some therapeutic way to complete the piece as a sort of tribute to Christopher. He now considers the sketch – 'The Twinkle Dolls', a parody of the seaside concert party shows – to be one of the best he has ever written and it was actually included on the long playing record of *Beyond Our Ken*.

Dad was also contracted to write material for Norman Vaughan, the compère of the live variety show *Sunday Night at the London Palladium*, and I have very vivid memories of the Sunday morning rehearsals to which I would sometimes accompany him. I suppose I must have had the most star-studded autograph book for my age because performers such as Bob Hope, Sammy Davis Jr, Judy Garland, Ella Fitzgerald and other world famous celebrities appeared on the show.

My dad was not, however, the first Merriman to be involved in radio recordings, as his father was Percy Merriman, who during the First World War founded and wrote songs and sketches for 'The Roosters', a concert party troupe. The Roosters were actually amongst the first performers to broadcast on radio. In November 1930, Percy was reported as saying, 'There were no tests then, no palaver, no contracts, no rehearsals to speak of – the announcer simply said, "There's the microphone and good luck!"' He recalled junior members of the BBC staff pouring water from jugs into basins to suggest a rippling stream. Some things, you see, just don't change.

The show business connection also extends to my maternal grandmother, who hailed from Edinburgh. Kitty Robie was quite a well-known music hall singer whose billing was 'The Woman with the Fascinating Arms'. I've never been quite able to work this one out, although I've been told that, at the turn of the century, elbows were considered quite erotic. The thought of my grandmother flexing her triceps and sending young men in the Glasgow Empire into paroxysms of ecstasy is one to savour – but only momentarily . . .

My attempts to tread the boards were much less successful,

although when I was a very small boy I actually did some commercials for magazines, newspapers and on television. Unfortunately, I started to become camera shy at the age of five and my mother decided that it wasn't a good idea to continue. So, apart from participating in a few crowd scenes in a couple of radio productions, I've been 'resting' ever since.

The idea for the fourth generation of Merrimans to be involved in radio came when Sarah was about six months old. I had initially kicked around some thoughts about a situation comedy based on Sarah with an actor friend of mine, Paul Kelly, who is Sarah's godfather. We worked on a few ideas, but in due course Paul understandably decided that the subject was really too personal for his involvement and would be more aptly written by the immediate members of the family.

I had been collaborating with Dad for about five years and together we had enjoyed some success on radio with a couple of series for Richard Griffiths, *Mr Finchley Takes the Road* and *Mr Finchley Goes to Paris*, which were based on the novels by Victor Canning. When I suggested to him that we now try to create a situation comedy about a family with a child who has Down's syndrome, his first reaction was one of disbelief. How could we possibly be humorous about a subject like this? We had only just come to terms with the shock of it all and now we were going to make jokes about her? I assured him that the jokes would not be at Sarah's expense, but that the element of drama would be just the sort of thing that TV and radio were looking for.

I have to make it clear that during my dad's heyday, such issues would not have been considered suitable to be dealt with in a 'comedy' show and all language was very strictly vetted to protect the audience from any embarrassing vulgarity. Even the word 'keyhole' was banned from the radio airwaves and was included in the famous blue book of unmentionable words. 'Keyhole' used in any context – not just in the insidious matter of voyeurism – was considered to be highly indecent and suggestive and could only be interpreted in a licentious way.

The dear listeners of middle England were thus protected from any situation that might cause any moral offence and, in a way, I think the BBC were right. Just think, if things had not changed we might never have been subjected to Lloyd Grossman's television programme, *Through the Keyhole* – it might have been Lloyd Grossman's *Left on the Doorstep* and we would have all no doubt been very grateful. Since then, of course, we have come a long way in terms of acceptable phrases and vocabulary although there are still the odd examples of eccentric regulation. On radio, for example, one 'cannot use the word bugger' unless it is said with a North Country accent. Then it is deemed to be the vernacular and therefore broadcastable. Nation shall speak peace unto Nation – but only with a certain inflection.

Initially, the principal reason for writing the show was thus professional and it was an attempt to combine humour and drama. Whilst we were addressing a serious subject, it was not meant to be a show about Down's syndrome, but it was to be about a family who happen to have a child with Down's syndrome. We were certainly desperate to avoid being preachy or patronizing the audience, but of course if the dramatic text provided some information and, more importantly, exploded some of the myths about Down's syndrome then this would be an added bonus.

We were encouraged with the idea and then commissioned by Jonathan James-Moore, the head of Radio Light Entertainment, to write a pilot script. We were keen to work again with Gareth Edwards, who had produced the Mr Finchley series so beautifully, and we recorded the pilot in March 1996. It was actually Gareth's idea to use Sarah in the show to play the part of Amy as he thought that it would create the right atmosphere and that the actors would respond well to a real toddler in the studio.

Surprisingly, I hadn't actually thought of this and had assumed that he would use pre-recordings of a child's voice or sound effects where necessary.

Of course, once the series was commissioned, and we knew that Sarah would be featured more than originally envisaged, we gave her more dialogue and we devoted more time to the plots involving her. In fact, someone purporting to be her agent, but I think was a grandparent, threatened to pull her out of the show unless we re-wrote her material!

Although I did put my daughter on the stage, I certainly didn't intend for this series to be Sarah's big break into acting and we made sure that she wasn't exploited in any way. The BBC are quite rightly extremely careful about the use of children in productions and adhere zealously to the strict guidelines about the number of hours that can be worked, mealtimes and educational input. Gareth and his marvellous production assistant, Carol Smith, were very diligent in this matter and Sarah had her very own professional chaperone in the form of my mother, Jean Merriman, who has worked in this field for many years. In order to seek gainful employment, Sarah had to have a licence and a medical certificate to verify that she was fit to work.

Sarah and I thus trooped off to the local surgery with an appointment to see a locum doctor. He was quite bewildered as to why we were there, as she didn't appear to be unwell. I explained the need for a medical certificate and following his initial confusion, he suddenly turned into a medical Esther Rantzen. He was delighted that such strict measures were taken to prevent the exploitation of children and grilled me for a good half an hour about what was expected of Sarah. I assured him that there was no question of her being exploited and that, in any case, I would be at all the recordings to ensure that she was happy and looked after properly. 'Oh that doesn't mean anything,' he replied. 'You know about these star-struck parents –

they'll do anything to see their children made famous. You can't always rely on the parents.'

If I'd been sending Sarah up chimneys, I couldn't have felt worse and hoped that other people wouldn't be so suspicious about my motives. He finally handed me the letter, which stated that Sarah 'is suffering from Down's syndrome, but she is fit to be involved in radio recording'.

Life is full of coincidences which we usually regard as the result of pure and random chance. The psychiatrist and psychotherapist Carl Jung held the view that although coincidence exists, there is also another principle at work; he called this synchronicity and defined it as coincidences connected so meaningfully that their chance occurrence would be incredible. There have been a couple of extraordinary instances in regard to *Minor Adjustment* that have almost converted me to the idea of 'synchronicity'.

When it has come to casting our radio shows, we have always been fortunate in the producer being sympathetic to our ideas and when Dad and I suggested Peter Davison for the part of Amy's father, Richard Stubbs, Gareth immediately agreed. We all thought that Peter was a most talented and natural actor with the sort of sensitivity that the character possessed. It was only after Peter had accepted the role that I discovered that he was a patron of the Down's Syndrome Association and undertook a lot of work on their behalf! We were thus delighted not only to have such a well-known and clever performer as Peter in the show, but also that he had great understanding and awareness of learning disability.

The other even more inexplicable parallel was that concerning the character of Amy's mother, who was named Sarah Stubbs and played in the series by Samantha Bond. We had recorded the pilot show and were awaiting a decision on the rest of the series when Sarah (our Sarah) had started to attend the local nursery school. The education department of Haringey Council had provided her with a special needs assistant who had since left and had been replaced by a colleague. On her first day, the new special needs assistant introduced herself to me.

'Hello, I'm Sarah Stubbs.'

'Pardon?' I said.

'Sarah Stubbs,' she repeated.

'There must be some mistake.'

'I don't think so.'

'No, you can't be,' I said.

'I am,' she said. 'Definitely.'

'No, no, no, you're a figment of my imagination,' I suggested.

'Unlikely.'

We were both completely perplexed and after another few minutes of discommodious conversation, she managed to convince me that she was indeed the original Sarah Stubbs! I was very relieved when she told me that her husband wasn't called Richard and although she had two children they were named Lindsey and Gary. It's lucky that Sarah is such a patient woman, as she must have thought I was utterly mad.

In all we made six episodes and we were lucky to have a terrific cast, including Claire Russell as Kate, Amy's teenage sister, Phyllida Law as Amy's grandmother and cameo performances by Peter Jones, Theresa Gallagher and Kerry Shale. Sarah's older brother Daniel also featured in the last episode as did Pius Hickey, a very talented actor who also happens to have Down's syndrome and is part of the Strathcona Theatre Company.

A special guest in one of the episodes was Bill Pertwee, an old friend of my dad's from the days of *Beyond Our Ken* and also my brother Christopher's godfather. Although best known for his role as the ARP warden in *Dad's Army*, Bill has a terrific range of voices. He is also a prolific writer and he was particularly complimentary about his involvement in our show in his engaging autobiography, *Funny Way to Make a Living*.

All the cast were wonderfully kind and patient with Sarah and Samantha Bond, who has two small children herself, spent a lot of time playing with and reading to Sarah. Samantha actually insisted on Sarah being in a number of scenes that we hadn't written her into. By the end of the series, Sarah was extraordinarily confident and on the day of the last recording strode into the studio, theatrically threw her bag on to the nearest chair and announced her arrival with a 'Hello everyone, I'm here.'

Once the project was in production, it seemed to develop a life of its own and the show created a great deal of media interest. We were featured in articles in the London *Evening Standard*, the *Hampstead and Highgate Express* and there was a particularly detailed and sensitive interview by Jan Barden which appeared in the *Mail on Saturday*.

Sarah, Peter Davison and I were also asked to appear on the *Good Morning* show with Richard Madeley and Judy Finnegan. We were to be flown to Manchester airport and then driven to Liverpool from where the show was then broadcast. I was rather concerned at how Sarah would cope with flying, which she had never done before, and then being subjected to the confines and paraphernalia of a television studio. Sarah actually loved the experience and was quite relaxed throughout the flight. When we told the crew and other passengers about our impending TV appearance, she was treated with celebrity status.

Shortly before we were about to go on, one of the researchers unadvisedly told me that over two million people watched this live broadcast. I was terrified, but this didn't seem to bother Sarah at all and being a good trouper, she performed admirably. The fact that I had her on my lap during the interview and that I had to keep her interest was both distracting and comforting! We also benefited from the calming influence of Peter Davison – an old hand at television interviews.

Peter was terrific in publicizing the show and is a wonderful ambassador for Down's syndrome. He made several more television and radio appearances and mentioned *Minor Adjustment* wherever possible in media interviews. Shortly after, Allie, myself, Daniel and Sarah were interviewed on the *After 5* programme by Karon Keating. I felt much less nervous this time and it was a great adventure for the family. Daniel's school friends were most impressed that he had spoken on live television and Karon Keating was extremely friendly, sensitive and warm. On the way home, the driver who collected us from the television studio told us that the previous day Marlon Brando had been a passenger in his car. 'Bit of a comedown for you to drive us now,' I told him. 'Not really,' he said. 'He's just another client and . . . in any case your family are a lot easier on my suspension.'

The show was also nominated for a 'Raspberry Ripple' award for positive portrayal of disability in the media and it was terrific to be involved in a televised event that actually addressed some of the issues of disability in radio, television, theatre and cinema.

The whole experience of being involved in *Minor Adjustment* was quite marvellous and very exciting for all the family. I hadn't realized that writing the show would be such a cathartic experience and I was able to laugh and joke about things with my dad that would have been impossible when Sarah was born. At that time, I had neither wanted nor felt the need to bare my soul, but by looking at another family, albeit of our creation, I found I was projecting my own thoughts and feelings into their fictitious personae and in turn reflecting on how I felt. This meant that writing some of the scenes proved quite painful as previously untapped emotions were brought to the surface. I suspect that I would have strongly denied that this was part of my motivation for writing the series at the outset, but looking back, it seems that I was combining both an artistic and therapeutic opportunity.

Allie was very enthusiastic about the show and was particularly elated that a subject so close to her heart was being aired in a way she fully approved of and was also being heard by thousands of people. She felt that the right messages were being put across in a gentle but effective way. Allie was also desperate to hear every detail of my account of the day's recording and the one day that she did spend at Broadcasting House, chaperoning Sarah, she found quite intriguing, having never been to a radio studio before. She was thrilled to meet the cast and was particularly flattered to be mistaken for another actress by Samantha Bond!

Daniel was delighted with his sister (although a little jealous of the attention) and when he made his acting debut in the last episode, took great pleasure in telling his friends about his role as 'the naughty boy at the party'. He rehearsed his part constantly and remembers his lines to this day!

Sarah was the family member who took it most in her stride and obviously felt it was entirely natural to star in a radio series, to be invited on television chat shows and to have her photograph featured in various journals. 'Me again,' she commented nonchalantly, as she saw her face beaming out of the local newspaper. I was so proud of Sarah and at the end of the series, Gareth Edwards bought her a present and sent her a card, which read, 'Here's a big "Thank You" to one of the most professional actresses we've ever worked with.'

It would also be true to say that she was probably the only one who wasn't potty-trained.

13. You've Got to Have Art

'Welcome to Holland' is a piece that seems to have passed into Down's syndrome folklore – certainly in the United States. Originally from a film, *Kids Like These*, it was written by Emily Perl Kingsley in 1987.

> I am often asked to describe the experience of raising a child with a disability – to try to help people who have not shared that unique experience to understand it, to imagine how it would feel. It's like this . . .
>
> When you're going to have a baby, it's like planning a fabulous vacation trip – to Italy. You buy a bunch of guidebooks and make your wonderful plans. The Colosseum. The Michelangelo David. The gondolas in Venice. You may learn some handy phrases in Italian. It's all very exciting.
>
> After months of eager anticipation, the day finally arrives. You pack your bags and off you go. Several hours later, the plane lands. The stewardess comes in and says, 'Welcome to Holland.'
>
> 'Holland?!?' you say. 'What do you mean, Holland?? I signed up for Italy! And I'm supposed to be in Italy. All my life I've dreamed of going to Italy.'
>
> But there's been a change in the flight plan. They've landed in Holland and there you must stay. The important thing is that they haven't taken you to a horrible, disgusting, filthy place, full of pestilence, famine and disease. It's just a different place.
>
> So you must go out and buy new guidebooks. And you must learn a whole new language. And you will meet a whole new group of people you would never have met . . . It's just a

different place. It's slower-paced than Italy, less flashy than Italy
. . . But after you've been there for a while and you catch your
breath, you look around . . . and you begin to notice that
Holland has windmills . . . and Holland has tulips. Holland even
has Rembrandts.

But everyone you know is busy coming and going from Italy
. . . and they're all bragging about what a wonderful time they
had there. And for the rest of your life, you will say, 'Yes, that's
where I was supposed to go. That's what I had planned.'

And the pain of that will never, ever go away . . . because the
loss of that dream is a very, very significant loss. But if you
spend your life in mourning the fact that you didn't go to Italy,
you may never be free to enjoy the very special, the very lovely
things . . . about Holland.

I'm not sure that this article would have the endorsement of the
Dutch tourist board, but it is, I think, a terrific analogy. Emily
Kingsley's son, Jason, has Down's syndrome and when he was
born in 1974, the family was advised to tell friends and relations
that he died in childbirth and then to have him institutionalized.

The parents were told that Jason would probably never recognize them, walk, talk or 'have any meaningful thoughts'. It must
have been something of a shock for these 'experts' to find a book
in bookshops and libraries twenty years later entitled *Count Us
In: Growing Up with Down Syndrome* written by Jason Kingsley
in collaboration with Mitchell Levitz, another young man who
has Down's syndrome. The book is based on over fifty conversations between the two lifelong friends, who describe their
thoughts, feelings and experiences of growing up with Down's
syndrome. It is a fascinating insight and related with great
honesty and charm.

Jason Kingsley writes with much pride about his life and is
understandably indignant about the fact that he could so easily

have been forsaken at birth. 'The obstetrician never imagined how I could write a book. I will send him a copy so he'll know . . . I will tell him that I play the violin, that I make relationships with other people, play the piano, I can sing, I am competing in sports . . . and I have a full life. He will never discriminate against people with disabilities again. And then he will be a better doctor.'

Five years before Jason was born, Emily Kingsley was employed as one of the original writers of *Sesame Street*, which was the first television programme to regularly feature children with Down's syndrome and other disabilities. Viewers of all ages became used to seeing these children actually being able to count, spell and play like other kids! Although this doesn't sound terribly radical now, nearly thirty years ago it was quite a breakthrough in mainstream programming. The success of *Sesame Street*, which is just as popular now as ever before, is due to the seemingly effortless and natural coupling of learning and entertainment. The inclusion of children with disabilities in the show has been an equally unaffected process.

Another autobiography, *Special Kind of Hero*, was written by actor Chris Burke, who has Down's syndrome and starred in an American television series, *Life Goes On. Life Goes On* is about a family with a teenage son who has Down's syndrome. The part of Corky was played by Chris Burke, who won a number of awards for his acting. Although the series does concentrate on Corky's character, it is also the story of a family having to cope with everyday problems. The show was a prime time success in the United States, but only shown here by a few ITV network channels and then only in an afternoon slot.

British television shows in recent years such as *Brookside* and *Casualty* have also had storylines using characters with Down's syndrome and the plot in an episode of *A Touch Of Frost* which stars David Jason, featured a man with Down's syndrome, played by Timmy Lang, who was wrongly accused of murder. The show was courageously written and addressed many of the preconceptions about adults with learning disabilities.

The major plotline of a 1998 episode of the medical drama *Peak Practice* related the story of a young man with Down's syndrome, played by Elliot Rosen, who needed a heart transplant, but was refused to be considered for the surgery by an unsympathetic hospital consultant. The patient's devoted brother and their sensitive GP battled with the authorities to at least have the case discussed and they did eventually overcome the hospital's prejudices. It was a well-written piece and the relationship between the two brothers was both natural and moving. We didn't ever discover how far the application proceeded, but if he had been accepted for a transplant it would have made British medical history. I suppose that would be taking 'poetic licence' a little too far!

An Australian television series, *House Gang*, is set in a group home and features two adults with Down's syndrome and endeavours to challenge the conventional representation and roles of disabled in the media. In the last episode of the first series, the show tackled the subject of sex education and the characters talked openly and frankly about sex, relationships and the intimate experiences they had enjoyed. This episode apparently caused quite an outcry in the outback where there were numerous complaints about the content of the show. Although it was all pretty innocuous, the clear implication is that adults with disabilities – even fictional – should not be encouraged to talk about sex, never mind have it. It's OK for adults with Down's syndrome to be affectionate as long as it doesn't lead to its natural conclusion.

There have been a number of films – *One Flew Over the Cuckoo's Nest*, *My Left Foot* and *Rain Man* – during the last couple of decades which have addressed the notion of disability

Sarah and Andy Merriman.
(Peter Rosenbaum/Daily Mail)

Sarah, Andy and Eric Merriman.
(BBC/Chris Capstick)

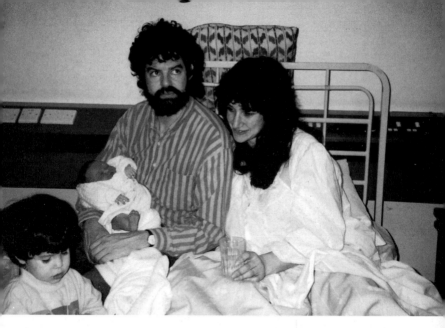

The Merriman family, hours after Sarah's birth…
and with baby Joel and Jean Merriman, five years later. Sarah was an enthusiastic
bridesmaid at her producer's wedding. *(Wedding photograph; Peter Morfoot)*

The Merriman family playing at
home in London…

… and away in Suffolk.

Clockwise from top left:
Detail from Robin Hood Bay by *Sally Johnson (Down's Syndrome Association)*.
Antonia 1996 by *Rachel Heller*. Mother and Child, Deborah and India Hope Russell,
by *Norman Douglas Hutchinson*. Sarah, painted by seven-year-old *Daniel* in 1996.

Sarah and Daniel Merriman, 1994.

Allie and Sarah Merriman, 1996.

Sarah and Joel keep house, 1998.

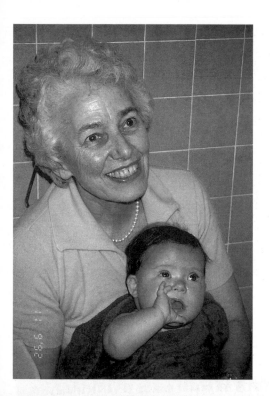

Baby Sarah is held by her grandmother, Ursula, and four years later reads with her grandfather, John.

The cast of *Minor Adjustment*.
Peter Davison, Clare Russell, Sarah Merriman and Samantha Bond.
(BBC/Chris Capstick)

and the Oscar laden *Forrest Gump* is probably the most well known of these movies. Despite some of its rather conservative attitudes and excess of deaths, I must say that it moved me and did, I think, have some effect on general attitudes. Gump's unique philosophy and an ability to take in everything so literally creates a character of empathy who wishes to bestow pure kindness upon everyone he meets. The film attempts to show that the relationship between intelligence and achievement isn't necessarily symbiotic. As Forrest Gump himself says, 'Stupid is as stupid does.'

Until 1996, however, there hadn't been a major cinematic work featuring a character with Down's syndrome. A Belgian actor with Down's syndrome, Pascal Duquenne, co-starred in the film *The Eighth Day* and shared the Best Actor prize at the Cannes film festival with his co-star Daniel Auteuil. Pascal Duquenne has worked in a travelling theatre group for ten years and according to his more illustrious co-star is 'a genuinely fine and truthful actor'.

The story follows the unusual relationship between two lost souls. Harry (Auteuil) is a businessman whose obsession with work has now cost him his marriage and he is in search of his daughters who went missing when his marriage failed. He meets Georges (Duquenne), who is an escapee from an institution and on a quest to find his mother. He does not know or cannot accept the fact she has died some years earlier.

The film is powerful and moving and treats Georges in a profound and insightful manner. He is not there just as a foil to the lead character and is a personality in his own right. It is to the credit of the director, Jaco Van Dormael, that the film has successfully attempted to highlight the prejudices surrounding Down's syndrome without patronizing or moralizing.

A recent successful British film, *Shooting Fish*, a witty feelgood comedy starring Stuart Townshend, Dan Futterman and Kate

Beckinsale, also featured a character with Down's syndrome played by Darren Renouf. Other actors and extras with Down's syndrome were chosen from the Kaleidoscope Theatre company.

The silver screen is not, of course, the first medium in which depictions of people with Down's syndrome have appeared. There were others earlier – much earlier in fact.

The Olmecs were a tribe of Indians who lived in the Gulf of Mexico from about 1500 BC to AD 300 and according to Brian Stratford, in the extraordinarily informative *New Approaches to Down Syndrome*, the discovery of carvings, figurines and sculptures seems to represent adults with Down's syndrome existed. A series of wall reliefs suggests that the presence of children with Down's syndrome was the result of mating between women of the tribe with the jaguar, the sacred totem of the Olmecs. These children were thus treated as products of the gods and therefore 'sacred hybrids'.

So, if Sarah had been born a few thousand years ago in another continent, she may have been treated as a 'sacred hybrid'. Judging by some of her more demanding behaviour on occasions, she must already know about this!

Brian Stratford also goes on to discuss artists of the Renaissance and describes how Andrea Mantegna (1431–1506) was one of the first artists to use living people as models for his paintings. One of his works, *Madonna and Child*, is exhibited at the Uffizi museum in Florence. It was created whilst he was the court painter for the rich and powerful Gonzaga family in fifteenth century Mantua and the child undoubtedly has Down's syndrome.

Angels surrounding the *Madonna della Humilita* painted about 1437 by the Carmelite friar Filippo Lippi have certain characteristics of Down's syndrome and the Flemish artist, Jacob Jordaens (1593–1678), had a daughter with Down's syndrome who featured in some of his paintings. I'm relieved that I wasn't the first father to employ his daughter to further a professional career!

One of Sarah's greatest friends is India Hope Russell. India, who is a year younger than Sarah, also has Down's syndrome. Although she and her family have now moved to Warwickshire and the two girls do not see as much of each other as they would like, there is always great excitement when we visit or India comes to stay. India and Sarah are wonderful together and I'm sure will enjoy a long and fruitful friendship.

We have always wanted Sarah to be fully integrated and have friends from a wide spectrum, but there is something special about their relationship – a kind of mutual awareness and understanding of their situation. Sarah will, at some point, want to understand more about her identity and this will involve knowing and being close to other people with Down's syndrome.

India's mother, Deborah Russell, is an artist as is her grand-father, Norman Douglas Hutchinson. Soon after India was born, her grandfather painted a portrait of Deborah and India – *Mother and Child* in a modern style *Madonna and Child*. India is attired in a saffron robe and the painting, which is quite stunning, possesses a calm, zen-like quality.

The link between Down's syndrome and art does not, of course, exist purely in the representational sense. There are a couple of extremely talented contemporary artists with Down's syndrome, who have made their names in the art world in the last few years.

Rachel Heller is a twenty-three-year-old woman who has made an extraordinary impact on the art world in the last few years. Described by the art critic Edward Lucie-Smith as wholly orig-inal, and someone who has 'reinvented the meaning of the life-class . . . with a purity of intention which very few artists manage to attain', Rachel also fulfilled another achievement which very few other artists manage to attain – she sold out her first two exhibitions!

I went to see Rachel and discovered that music plays an equally important part in her life – her drum kit dominates a spare bedroom and she plays the trumpet and piano. However, she needed little prompting to show me her studio – a disused garage at the family home, which was littered with her drawings, etchings and pieces of pottery.

Obviously influenced by the family's artistic background – her mother is gallery owner Angela Flowers and her father, management consultant and author Bob Heller – Rachel soon developed an interest in and awareness of art. Even as a young girl, her parents were keen to imbue her with an appreciation of art and Rachel always accompanied them to exhibitions and galleries. Every available area of wall space in the family home is covered with works of art and Rachel's bedroom is festooned by a large number of paintings. Rachel started to draw at a very early age and following an invitation from the Byam School of Art, she began to attend life classes on Saturday mornings. Her first show soon followed.

Rachel produces striking portraits in a style that is clearly personal and the movement in the drawings and etchings is remarkable. Spontaneity and lack of inhibition are major components of her drawings and yet Rachel combines these natural skills with sheer dedication. This is particularly interesting because an inability to concentrate is supposedly a characteristic of people with Down's syndrome. Rachel possesses a single-minded determination to focus on her work and she has a zealous regard for her craft. She spends two days a week visiting various museums and galleries and has been known to sit for hours producing copies of well-known paintings.

Fellow artist and friend John Kirby says, 'Rachel's work has reached an extraordinary maturity and beauty. She appears to understand instinctively how a figure works within the composition of a drawing and she accentuates and isolates elements which add to the power and sensuality of the piece.'

Rachel can read and write well, but does have some problems with her speech, lacking the confidence to attempt more difficult vocabulary. Like many other people, Rachel expresses herself fluently in other forms of communication. Her art speaks volumes.

Sally Johnson first came to our attention soon after Sarah was born, as her watercolours are used by the Down's Syndrome Association for their Christmas cards and calendars. Sally started to sketch and paint about eight years ago when accompanying her parents on trips to the Yorkshire moors. Her father, Ken, who died four years ago, was a professional artist and her mother, Sheila, is a keen sketcher. Sally realized that she, too, would like to draw and decided one day to take her own sketch pad on their outings.

Sally paints every day and her landscapes – obviously influenced by the Impressionists whom she adores – are fresh, passionate and full of light and beauty. She has two permanent exhibitions in Yorkshire and all the profits from her artwork go to the Down's Syndrome Association or other charities, although it is fair to say that Sally could make a living from selling her paintings – at least she could from me because I bought three on my visit!

Sally's artistic doctrine – the Impressionists were considered to be visionaries and anarchists in their time – is reflected in her inspirational lifestyle. She is now twenty-three and is an outgoing, articulate and funny young woman with myriad interests and hobbies. She has many friends, helps to run quizzes and games for the local youth club, has achieved a Gateway Gold Award (Mencap's [The Royal Society for Mentally Handicapped Children and Adults] equivalent to the Duke of Edinburgh award scheme), assists once a week at an old people's home, takes an active interest in current affairs, writes regular journals of her experiences and she had just finished reading *Villette* by Charlotte Brontë, when I went to see her.

This is all quite extraordinary – not because she has Down's syndrome but because of the medical reaction to her birth. Sally was not placed in her mother's arms, but was dumped in a cot at the end of the bed and the doctor announced, 'Well, Mrs Johnson, you've got a mongol.' When Sheila Johnson asked for some information about Down's syndrome – something to read so she could learn about the syndrome – she was told, 'Oh no. Don't do that, it's all too depressing.' Worse was to follow. Ten days after her birth, the Johnsons' then GP advised them about Sally. 'She'll be the village idiot, walking down the street, making hideous sounds, drooling and dribbling. Get rid of that child.'

This, believe it or not, was 1974 – not the Victorian age when one might sadly expect this sort of ignorance. This 'advice' – let's face it, the physician's bedside manner lay closer to Dr Crippen's than Dr Finlay's – was fortunately completely ignored by Mr and Mrs Johnson. In fact his lack of sensitivity hardened their resolve to treat their desperately wanted daughter like any other child.

Sheila, a primary school teacher, realized the significance of education for Sally and battled with the local primary school to accept her and then for nearly three years with the education authority to obtain a place for Sally at a school for the physically 'handicapped' (Sally also has physical disabilities) where she knew Sally would be stimulated and achieve her full potential.

In her early years, Sally was discriminated against by the medical profession who were clearly disinterested in her because she had Down's syndrome and felt that she was not worth bothering with. Sally has a serious heart and lung condition which was not diagnosed until she was four. If this condition had been diagnosed earlier it could have been reversed. As it is, Sally is dependent on oxygen when she goes out, can only walk very short distances, and has on several occasions been given only months to live. Her mother has to accompany her everywhere – a situation that is frustrating for both Sally and her mother who wishes her to be as independent as possible.

Sally has inherited her mother's tenacity and describes herself as having 'a fighting spirit' which has helped her throughout her life. Sally and Sheila have an extraordinarily close and honest relationship and remain happy and optimistic. When Sally was the subject of a short television programme which documented her life and explained her interests, hobbies and lifestyle, she received a number of letters from other young women who said they now felt unfulfilled and wanted to emulate Sally.

It is because of parents like Sheila Johnson, who fought against all the odds at a time when it would have been much easier to yield to all the external pressures, that children like Sarah are now benefiting.

We are in great debt to them all.

Of course I am biased, but I am drawn to creative people and because of Sarah, creative people with Down's syndrome are like magnets. The dedication to their art – whichever form it takes – is resolute. As George Bernard Shaw said, 'The true artist will let his wife starve, his children go barefoot, his mother drudge for his living at seventy, sooner than work at anything but his art.' I do not want to suggest that all people with Down's syndrome are exceptionally talented, but like everyone else, they must be given the encouragement to express their art.

14. Screening From Sight

There is an Aborigine tribe that believes that their children choose their future parents by hiding behind huge rocks and surreptitiously viewing prospective mothers and fathers. When the most suitable adults pass by, the babies leap out and grab them, thereby claiming their family birthright. Similar conjecture is sometimes insinuated when describing the parents of children with Down's syndrome.

It is thus suggested that somehow you have been chosen to care for this child because only you could manage this terrible burden. It is perhaps a way of people trying to say something 'nice' in that the child couldn't possibly have better parents. It is karma or fate and either the child has chosen you, or God, in his infinite wisdom, decided to send you 'a little angel' as a 'special gift'. Of course this doesn't really address the issue of those children who 'chose' their parents and were given up for adoption, institutionalized, neglected and abused. It certainly doesn't explain why some children with Down's syndrome opt for parents who then decide to have them terminated.

The first question that some people asked when told about Sarah having Down's syndrome was, 'Did you have any tests?' Allie did have a blood test which measures the levels of Alpha Feta Protein and indicates certain disorders, but the result was actually more 'normal' than when she had the same test with Daniel two years previously. We didn't request an amniocentesis (a sample of amniotic fluid is removed and tested) because we had no reason to believe that there would be any complications with the birth of our second child and in any case Allie was below the age when it is offered automatically. I now dread to think what may have happened if we had known the baby had Down's syndrome because our prejudices and fears may well have influenced us to consider a termination.

Many women who choose not to undergo any pre-natal screening and subsequently have babies with Down's syndrome are often very relieved that they didn't opt for an amniocentesis. The likelihood is that faced with such a difficult decision, they may well have decided to terminate. Let's face it, if you are told that your baby may never grow up to read and write, lead a normal life and that he or she is destined for unfulfilment and unhappiness, may suffer a heart defect, that there is a higher risk of leukaemia and later Alzheimer's, then it is likely that you will choose not to continue the pregnancy.

Routine diagnostic testing for Down's syndrome, which is the most common abnormality that can be diagnosed by pre-natal testing, is offered in most areas to mothers of all ages and often little or no counselling is given. Medical staff often assume termination will be the automatic choice if the baby the mother is carrying has Down's syndrome.

In a 1996 National Childbirth Trust survey of 2,722 women who had undergone pre-natal screening, it was found that only just over half had received all the information and support that they needed. Some health professionals made assumptions that screening and termination of the pregnancy was in the parents' best interests if the baby had a disability and appointments were booked for amniocentesis without prior discussion. Some women were tested without consent or some given inappropriate tests and in some cases women were being refused an amniocentesis unless they agreed to terminate the pregnancy if Down's syndrome was detected.

Nearly half the women were not given a follow up telephone number if they did have any concerns and the most frequent complaint was the lack of opportunity in obtaining full information about the tests and the possible consequences.

In 1997 an Audit Commission report on maternity services in England and Wales stated, 'Many ante-natal tests carry a range of potential problems for women and their families, including psychological and emotional ones. Like any screening tests, they miss some cases and raise false alarms, sometimes giving uncertain results that require further tests. They therefore have the potential to cause great anxiety.'

As a result of this anxiety, the Down's Syndrome Association is contacted by over 250 women a month who have had a pre-natal test of some kind, requesting information that ante-natal clinics or other professionals have failed to provide.

There are now two basic types of test available – diagnostic and screening. The screening tests – mainly blood tests and ultrasound scans – provide only an estimate of the possibility of the baby having Down's syndrome and do not allow a firm diagnosis to be made. The results are thus uncertain and each test possesses its own percentages and odds. A foetal lottery where it really could be you.

The two main available diagnostic tests are amniocentesis and CVS (Chorionic Villus Sampling) – where tissue is taken from the placenta – to identify Down's and other chromosomal abnormalities and both carry a risk of miscarriage between approximately 1 and 2 per cent.

The above procedures can thus actually have a higher statistical risk of causing miscarriage than a thirty-six-year-old woman has of carrying a baby with Down's syndrome. It is then a stark choice between a miscarriage or giving birth to a child with Down's syndrome and yet again parents are left to take their chances.

It is quite clear that the expectation from health professionals is that you will have a termination if your foetus is abnormal.

The experience of testing should be about a decision to prepare for the birth of your child or to terminate – not just as precursor to an inevitable abortion. Parents must be given realistic information not advice based on ignorance and prejudice.

I am not against abortion and would not like to ally myself with the pro-life lobby. The notion put forward by these groups that there is an army of suitable adoptive parents desperate to get their hands on a 'rewarding', 'happy', 'affectionate' baby with Down's syndrome is, I'm afraid, a myth. I know of a number of babies with Down's syndrome given up at birth, who have waited months and years for adoption by *suitable* families (not by families who already have two, three or even more children with Down's syndrome – a situation which I think is just the antithesis of integration).

I still believe that 'every child does have to be a wanted child', but I am concerned that parents are making decisions without knowing all the facts about Down's syndrome. The choice must be informed – made from knowledge not ignorance and all aspects of the positive alternative to termination must be discussed. I do also object to the supposition that any child who is not 'perfect' will not be wanted and therefore disposed of.

Professor Kypros Nicolaides of Kings College Hospital is at the forefront of screening, but admits that there are inadequate counselling resources. 'We are frustrated by the lack of funding.' He doesn't seem to have any trouble funding more and more ways of screening for disability. It is he who has perfected the Nuchal Transluscency Scan, which measures fluid at the back of the foetus's neck and indicates whether there is a likelihood of Down's.

Pre-natal technology has become and continues to be more and more sophisticated and more adept at eliminating Down's syndrome. There is no doubt that the increasing availability of tests to detect the chromosomal abnormality has influenced people and actually feeds people's fears and prejudices. Although there is supposedly a greater awareness of disability in general, if people constantly read about and are told of the effects to rid society of Down's syndrome, their attitudes to adults who have Down's syndrome are unlikely to be very positive.

Tracey Burke of West Suffolk won £12,000 compensation after she aborted a healthy baby following a test mix-up after a mislabelling of samples at Addenbrooke's Hospital in Cambridge. The hospital admitted the mistake and newspaper reports referred to the 'horror of the abortion of the healthy baby'. Down's syndrome is neither an illness, nor a disease and yet from these reports we are led to believe this is the case. Thus, the termination of a baby with Down's syndrome is seen as an expectation and could not possibly be described as 'horrific'. Where is the outrage about babies with Down's syndrome being terminated just because they happen to have an extra chromosome?

Another story that made the headlines in 1997 was that of Sandra Hurley, who was awarded £300,000 in a High Court damages claim. Mrs Hurley gave birth to a baby with Down's syndrome, having been refused an amniocentesis by a doctor at a Ministry of Defence Hospital. Mrs Hurley was quoted as saying, 'If I'd had the test, I wouldn't have gone through with the pregnancy. Now, he's here, I love him with all my heart and wouldn't be without him.'

Whilst I cannot blame Mrs Hurley for wanting to obtain financial security for her son's future – it certainly doesn't harm to have a tidy sum put aside for your children's dotage – it creates a disability market place. What price an undetected baby with spina bifida? Is the tariff on an aborted foetus with Down's syndrome now higher than an aborted foetus in the Burke case? The main problem with stories like this is that it perpetuates the idea that giving birth to a baby with Down's syndrome is the worst possible thing that can happen to any parent. The most telling comment, in fact, came from an MoD spokesman, who said, 'We never comment on settlements, least of all where tragedies like Down's syndrome are concerned.' Tragedy . . . oh really? I must remind Sarah that she is nothing more than a tragedy waiting to grow up.

With the advance of medical technology the number of children born with Down's syndrome is likely to fall dramatically in the coming years, until there are very few people like Sarah around. Those remaining will become incredibly isolated and their parents are going to find it increasingly difficult to accept and cope with their disability.

In the United States, billions of dollars have been spent in trying to detect abnormalities in blood cells as early as possible in the pregnancy and in Britain, clinicians are looking into obtaining foetal cells from the cervix during the first trimester of pregnancy. Whilst there are some advantages for early and less invasive tests and that women may have longer to consider all the options, there is no doubt that early terminations are more likely to be encouraged.

There is also a question of how much money is spent on these screening methods when some of the huge sums could be spent on medical research or more resources and facilities for those with Down's syndrome who actually exist. One might hope that we could try to maximize the potential of children and adults with Down's syndrome rather than weed them out and destroy them before they are born.

The fiscal argument or 'cost benefit analysis' does have a large influence on the way forward for the medical profession. Researchers at St Bartholomew's Hospital felt that it would be 'cost effective' to screen all women for Down's syndrome – not just those over the age of thirty-five, as was the case up until the last few years. They estimated that 'it costs approximately £38,000 to avoid one Down's baby' and compared this to the lifetime costs of caring for one child with Down's syndrome.

The market economy distinguishes between 'productive and unproductive' citizens and there is a possibility in the near future

– if we haven't already reached it – that, as Michael Bérubé says, 'People who choose to bear disabled children will be considered selfish, deluded or irresponsible.' As I mentioned earlier, there is an obvious parallel to 1930s Germany when the 'mentally handicapped' were seen to be a financial drain on able-bodied citizens. This link was highlighted by Dominic Lawson, now the editor of the *Sunday Telegraph*, when his daughter, Domenica, was born with Down's syndrome. In a well publicized article which he wrote barely two weeks after her birth, he described the eugenic connection. 'An industry has been developed to make it increasingly improbable that children like Domenica will be allowed to live . . . this is nothing less than state sponsored annihilation of viable, sentient foetuses.'

About one child in thirty is born with a genetic problem of some kind. Genetic engineering may enable us to discover and counteract human diseases and disabilities that are caused by a single gene or set of genes. Genetic links have been established with many disorders and in the future, we might be able to decide we don't want a deaf baby, a blind baby, a baby that might grow up to be fat, bald or those who are considered a drain on our medical resources such as alcoholics and smokers. Let's stamp out anyone who isn't 'normal' or who might be proved to be 'unproductive'.

Society is obsessed with the fact that we should all conform to the notion of 'normality'. Instead of trying to create a world where anything unconventional is looked upon with suspicion and fear, we should be trying to accept people's individuality and welcome those who are different.

I do not believe that Down's syndrome should be a sole reason for termination. None of the pre-natal tests can predict how able or disabled a child will turn out to be and what these children can eventually achieve. Most importantly, the tests cannot predict the quality of life. As Brian Wilson, Member of Parliament, a government minister and father of Eoin, who has Down's syndrome, explains, 'It's not an unusual expectation that society should offer this small number of people the best chance to fulfil their potential and guarantee their families support and consideration ... It is the endless drudgery of fighting for basic rights which causes far more distress than bearing a child with Down's syndrome.'

15. Relatively Speaking

A Grandfather's experience *by John Wellemin*

By the time our younger daughter Alison and her husband Andy were expecting their second baby, my wife Ursula and I were grandparents three times over; our elder daughter Carey and her husband Mike had two boys – Tom aged three and Nicky aged one – and Alison and Andy already had Daniel who was just over two years old.

We had no reason to expect anything out of the ordinary as Alison had a normal pregnancy previously and so I looked forward to the birth of our fourth grandchild with equanimity. So when in the early morning of 9 January Andy telephoned with the news that Alison had given birth to a bonny girl and that both were well, it was no surprise to me. I thought how lucky I was to have a new granddaughter to complement the three grandsons who gave us so much pleasure.

Ursula and I had to go out early that morning and we gave the good news to everyone we met. Shortly after returning home we received a further telephone call from Andy's mother who informed us that the latest news from the hospital was that the baby had Down's syndrome. I was not well up on the various forms in which Down's syndrome manifested itself and how different people can be affected in very different ways. In my mind's eye I saw a group of eight- to ten-year-olds dressed in dowdy clothes shuffling along a path in the park with very limited language and with no one making an effort to do anything to develop their abilities. All this just flashed through my mind while listening to the telephone call. I was also vaguely aware that a number of Down's syndrome children had serious heart defects and suffered from other physical disabilities and illnesses as a result of carrying the extra chromosome.

Ursula reacted just as I would have expected her to. On minor issues she often gets very excited and makes major problems out of them, but when it comes to a real crisis, she keeps very calm and collected. After a subsequent visit to the Whittington Hospital, she looked out a number of her medical books – she had lots of them, being a retired physiotherapist – and we studied the various references to Down's syndrome which gave us a better idea about what we had to expect in the future.

Certainly we did not feel there was much to celebrate. One of the first decisions I had to make was whether to do my usual videoing of the new baby. I decided to act as I had with the other three grandchildren and try to be as cheerful as possible without being unrealistic.

We drove over to Archway and, with some trepidation, entered the maternity wing. As we went in, we came across Alison and the baby being wheeled from the delivery room to the post-natal ward. Alison had been allocated a side room which gave more privacy. All our congratulations and small talk felt a little artificial and my feelings for Alison and Andy and the baby were more of sorrow than joy. To my mind and with all my 'knowledge' of Down's syndrome, she looked so vulnerable in Alison's arms athough, I guess, in reality she was no more so than any other baby a few hours after birth.

A few minutes later, Andy, Daniel and Jean (Andy's mother) arrived and the strained atmosphere was not relieved by taking videos and photographs of Sarah with various members of the family. Sarah behaved as any other baby and her looks were not so different either. We talked to each other with forced joviality, not daring to mention the fears all of us had for the future.

I had the desire to talk to someone freely about my real

concerns and, as I did so often, I sat down at my computer to write to my best friend Honza in Prague to whom I opened my heart; this made me feel more composed. We also had the task of informing a number of friends of the birth of Sarah and, the coward that I am, I left most of this to Ursula.

Over the next few weeks we had reports from various doctors and specialists who examined Sarah and, except for a hole between the two upper chambers of the heart, she was found to be healthy. There was even hope that this opening would close in time and even if it did not, we were told that it was not going to affect either the quality of her life or its length.

At the same time, one of my tennis partners' daughters-in-law also gave birth to a baby with Down's syndrome – in her case a boy. This baby was very badly affected and died after a few days. This did not help to reduce our worries about the future. The only aspect with which this family's situation helped me concerned the often aired view that the chance of having a baby with Down's syndrome increased steeply with age. Alison was nearly thirty-five years old when Sarah was born but my friend's daughter-in-law was only in her twenties which reassured me that no neglect or irresponsibility occurred in Sarah's birth. The interpretation of the statistics in this respect needed careful scrutiny. I suppose all of us look for reasons to rationalize certain events which defy rationalization.

Despite the fact that Sarah developed almost the same way as other babies, Ursula and I realized that much additional support would be required over the years to develop Sarah's skills and abilities to the maximum. It might mean additional physiotherapy, speech therapy, other medical assistance, teaching, etc., all of which would mean even more time and effort from Sarah's parents than are needed for other children. We therefore decided to try and do everything in our power to make it a little easier for Alison and Andy to cope with this situation.

Alison and Sarah spent only a short time in hospital and I

visited them there only once more before they went home. Seeing Sarah at home with her parents and brother made the situation seem more 'normal'. The aspect which struck me most over the first few months of Sarah's life was the obvious love Daniel displayed towards his sister. The tenderness with which he treated her surprised me. When a similar tenderness was shown also by Sarah's cousins, Tom and Nicky, I started wondering whether these very young children had an instinct that made them feel Sarah needed even more support than other babies.

This exceptionally strong bond between Sarah and Daniel has remained and has strengthened over time. Daniel is very supportive of Sarah and she obviously adores her older brother. It may be that I am comparing the relationship between Daniel and Sarah with that of Tom and Nicky, who are very close, but it is possible (and even likely) that the difference is not due to Sarah's slower development but the fact that in one case we are looking at the relationship between a boy and a younger sister whereas in the other case there are two boys, both of whom enjoy 'fighting'. And yet when Tom and Nicky are with Sarah, there is no fighting and they are extremely tender towards her.

It was interesting for me as a grandfather, who sees Sarah and Daniel only once or twice a month on average, to see the rapid change in Sarah. There is clearly a certain familial physical resemblance between Sarah and the rest of the family and she also has certain features which are common to most children with Down's syndrome. These latter features are more apparent under certain conditions, such as when Sarah is crying.

Sarah has developed into a sweet, loveable little girl who, however, has very much a mind of her own. I firmly claim that she is discerning in her choice of person on whom to bestow her affections. She has also got good taste – she and I get on very well!

For a grandfather it is important to be told by his grandchildren about their activities. Sarah was fairly late in developing understandable speech, although from a very young age she was able to make her wishes clear by an expressive face and using her hands. Since she has learned to speak there is no holding her back. When I telephone to speak to Alison or Andy, Sarah invariably insists on talking as well.

There were a number of important milestones in Sarah's life – first, to be accepted by a mainstream school where she seems to be a popular pupil and, more recently, the birth of her baby brother Joel, who is four years younger than Sarah. Although obviously some of the attention was diverted from Sarah to Joel, Sarah never showed the slightest tendency to jealousy and both she and Daniel are very gentle with Joel. It was Sarah who 'created' the name by which Joel is known within the family – Joely.

Most of the time when I am with Sarah I am oblivious that she has Down's syndrome as she is just my beloved granddaughter, Sarah. Yet the concern about how Sarah will develop over the next few decades remains – the difference between Sarah and other children of her age is very small at the moment, but how will that gap widen over the years? As a grandfather my greatest concern is that she should be happy whatever level of achievement she attains.

Letter to Sarah from Ursula Wellemin

Dear Sarah,   May 1997

Over five years ago when you were born and we heard that you had Down's syndrome, we were not happy. You were not what we expected and we did not know how you were going to develop.

I came to your house very often. What helped Mummy most about my visits was to talk and share her feelings with me about you. This helped me too.

I remember also having to talk to everyone about the fact that you had Down's syndrome in those early days and I even told a lady on the ski slopes in France!

We all tried to find out as much as we could about Down's syndrome. Your parents took you to various therapists and some came to your house. I was particularly interested to find out what physiotherapy would help you and, as a retired physiotherapist, I had a feeling of responsibility for it. However, I had never learned about Down's syndrome in my training or worked with a child like you.

I was privileged to watch a few special sessions you had with an Israeli physiotherapist when you were eight months old and when I used to visit every Monday, I tried to use some of the techniques that I had learned from her. I promise that some of those strenuous exercises I put you through were for your own good!

I followed your progress with the speech therapist and it was wonderful when you began to utter your first words. We learned Makaton together and do you remember how you loved watching the videotape of Dave Benson Phillips where he signed so beautifully whilst singing children's songs? We were so happy when you first learned to walk.

When you followed Daniel to nursery school, you settled in easily. You had lovely teachers – not least your special needs assistant, also named Sarah. Your teachers learned to sign specially for you. The first time I accompanied Mummy to nursery to fetch you was a treat for me and before going home, you picked up the picture you had painted that day.

Your speech is improving very well. Last week, an employee at the supermarket asked, 'Why aren't you at school today?' and you replied 'Because it's half-term.' I must stop being surprised by you!

Being a 'star-struck' grandma, I was thrilled when you took the part of Amy in the radio show, *Minor Adjustment*, and I could hear you performing on the radio. I was also delighted to be able to look after you during one of the recordings at Broadcasting House when your other grandma – your regular professional chaperone – couldn't come. I was so proud of you and everyone in the studio was so pleased with you. It was a wonderful experience for me.

Things have changed so much since those anxious times immediately after your birth. We have seen you grow up and develop and watched all the improvements with great pleasure. We are so happy with you, our lovely granddaughter. The description that fits you is 'charming', a word that is not usually in my vocabulary, but you inspire me to use it.

Don't let this go to your head.

Lots of love

Your Nannie Urs

Facade *by Jean Merriman*

The trouble with me is that I'm two-faced. My husband doesn't think so. He says I can't possibly be two-faced otherwise I'd never wear this one! But then he's a comedy writer, and that's the sort of remark I've come to accept as normal over the fifty years that we've been married.

What I mean to say is that outward appearances are deceptive. What you see is not necessarily what you get. Or, to put it another way, I don't wear my heart on my sleeve, although I know it is the right place. Sometimes on the surface I appear imperturbable, but I can assure you I'm not. Underneath I worry just like most people. The brave face is a facade. Don't ask me why. It's my nature. Always has been.

So when Sarah was born with Down's syndrome, I may have appeared unconcerned – but inwardly I suffered. I was as devastated as any of the family. But I felt that I needed to show strength and indeed encouragement to Andy, Alison and of course to my first grandchild, Daniel, on whom I doted. I wanted them to know that they had my whole-hearted support. And that whatever decisions they made, I would back them to the hilt.

It was especially difficult for me since I had always had two great fears where babies were concerned. Cot deaths and Down's syndrome. Both now haunted me. I lost our second son, Christopher, in a cot death at nine months. And here was the second. Lightning had struck twice.

But I mustn't show the inevitable emotions. So, when Andy and Alison decided – quite rightly, I have to say – to accept Sarah into the family circle, and do their best to help her to be as 'normal' as possible, I would of course go along with that. It did not come easily. In the early stages, as I cradled her in my arms, I did not feel the love and warmth that I should have done. Here was my new grandchild – slightly imperfect, a piece of porcelain that was chipped. Would I ever come to terms with it? But what was I worried about? That she wouldn't be like other children or that she looked so different? That people might stare and whisper denigrating remarks? No. I believe that most of the populace are now much more enlightened, sympathetic and kinder towards children with Down's syndrome.

Sarah is in mainstream school now and is helped by a special needs assistant. And the best thing is she loves school. She is bright and clever and she is becoming more and more adept physically. Sarah has faults naturally. She can be a bit greedy and demanding – especially if she doesn't get her own way or when she is seeking attention. But, isn't that just as true of any little child?

As I write, Sarah, is five years old. There is a long way to go and a lot for her parents to contend with. In fact, it is the future that is the main concern. I shall worry about the future. But, as I said at the beginning, I doubt if I shall ever show it.

Poetry in Emotion *by Eric Merriman*

Think me not rash
To copy Ogden Nash
And borrow for a while
His style
Of terse
Verse.

Her name is Sarah Kate
She's great
Even though
Dealt a strange blow
By fate.

So she has Down's
But don't send in the clowns
'Cos she herself is fun
Bringing sun
Into a world of grey
Where someday
A life she'll have to face
At her own pace.

In my fact-file
She's tactile
Loving and warm
True to form
Her almond eyes are no surprise
They're par for the course
Of course.

The clichés are true
She's musical too
Why else would a nice girl
Be such a hot 'Spice Girl'!

Alas her speech is hardly crisp
But spoken with a most engaging lisp
Occasionally a word
Is blurred
And some are bungled
As if she got her tang all tonguelled
Often she dabbles in babble
And when excited has the gift of the gabble.

Let's face it though she's only five
And has the look that says, 'I will survive'
She's not to blame
For being not the same
As others
Her brothers
Will take care
And share
Any of tomorrow's
Sorrows.

Meanwhile
Her so beguiling smile
Belies the fears
Of later years
And though we can't forget
The future isn't yet.
We must not think ahead
Instead
Enjoy her as she is

Uncork the fizz
For here's my simple toast
To Sarah
Who's fairer
And rarer
Than most.

Reactions of an Auntie *by Carey Philpott*

Girl or boy? Great excitement. I had just put down the telephone receiver to my parents who had told me that my sister, at full term of her pregnancy, was in labour. Soon afterwards, just before taking my eldest son, then aged three and a half years, to playgroup, they rang again. A baby girl. I was overjoyed. The first girl of the new generation in our family. At last a girl after my two boys, Tom and Nicholas, and Allie and Andy's son, Daniel. I was in high spirits as I waited for the playgroup doors to open and spread the good news to some of my friends.

I returned home with a light step and the telephone rang. It was Andy. 'Congratulations!' I shouted. A quiet voice answered, 'She has Down's syndrome.' I knew that Andy was good at telling jokes and being married myself to Mike, a man who loves to play practical jokes, I am really ashamed of my reaction. 'You are joking!' 'I wouldn't joke about that,' came the reply. 'I can't get through to your parents on the phone, so please can you let them know. Goodbye.'

I felt awful for two reasons. First, I was the most tactless, unsupportive sister-in-law in the world. More importantly, what kind of baby had my sister produced? There had been no signs during her pregnancy of anything wrong. I knew very little of Down's syndrome – they all have similar faces and haircuts and wear frumpy clothes with ankle socks and sandals. What will Mum and Dad say? What will all our futures bring?

I tried to telephone Mum and Dad. No reply. I paced up and down the house. I must protect my parents. I decided to tell them in person after collecting Tom from playgroup. My friend Sue, also collecting her son from playgroup, commented on my serious face. I told her the reason. She gave me a cuddle and burst into tears.

I arrived at Mum and Dad's house with both my children to

find that they had already been told the news. What could we do to help?

My mother offered us some lunch and my father drove the five of us to the Whittington Hospital. I felt very helpless and ignorant. The contrast between arriving at the joyous birth of Daniel just over two years ago and now was enormous. We first saw my little sister quietly sitting in the hospital corridor with a little bundle in her arms. (We later found out she was waiting for some tests on the baby.)

My sister is a very strong and brave person and she greeted us sadly. I felt at a loss about what to say but she broke the ice. She had been given her own room and we went to it. She talked and talked. Andy came into the room and paid some attention to my children. The rest of us had ignored them all day and he was trying to keep some sense of normality.

On the way home I bought a book on another family who had a Down's child. I desperately felt I needed more information on the syndrome.

The next few days were grim. What would the future hold for my new niece? Would she be able to live a 'normal' life? I felt encouraged by the book I had purchased. My sister had an insatiable appetite to talk about Sarah. Allie's background in psychology and counselling had taught her that she needed to talk to understand the situation she was in. Up to now her life had been relatively straightforward – this was the first real challenge that she had to meet.

That was over five years ago now. Today Sarah is a happy, extrovert, pretty child, and enjoys the same things as other children (and she makes friends quicker than most). Allie takes care that she is well dressed and has attractive haircuts. Looking back, she took slightly longer to become mobile and to talk than most children and she had a small hole in her heart which has now closed, but all children develop at their own speed and many have worse medical problems to overcome.

I have felt that Sarah has had more pressures on her than most children – she has been continually assessed from a young age while most children are not 'judged' until the age of seven in their school SATS tests. Sarah had to prove that she was capable of benefiting from mainstream education – most children automatically go!

I now feel an affinity with other children with Down's syndrome that I did not have before Sarah was born. The junior school that my son attends shares its site with a school for children with severe learning difficulties. Last year the two schools had a joint Christmas carol service. I was sitting opposite two children with Down's syndrome, who had similar features to Sarah (although she also has family resemblance). I felt these two children sitting opposite to me whom I did not know were members of my family.

I feel very optimistic about Sarah's future because I think her personality will help her achieve her objectives. I believe that children with Down's syndrome today have many more opportunities than those in the past, partly because they have help from specialists from a very young age. Also more attend mainstream schools and have extra help from welfare staff. We do not know where Sarah's abilities and limitations will lie when she is an adult but that equally applies to her brothers and cousins.

For me, the worst part of Sarah's Down's syndrome was my ignorance at the beginning. I wish that I would have known at the time how she would turn out by the age of five.

Cousin Sarah *by Tom Philpott (aged eight and three quarters)*

My first memory of Sarah was a tiny red-faced baby, snuggled up, helpless in my auntie's arms. I was three and a half at the time. I did not know anything was wrong with Sarah because I could not remember any other births (my brother is twenty-three months younger than me and my cousin Daniel fourteen months younger). Now I know Sarah has Down's syndrome but I do not notice it.

I think Down's syndrome is when the person does not learn as quickly as other people. They quite often look the same as each other as well as their family.

Sarah is my second oldest cousin (I now have five cousins) and I enjoy looking after her. The last time I went to her house I brought my viola. She had a go at scraping the bow. Sarah can be quite stubborn at times. When I asked her to return the bow she refused. I tried to stay calm, unsuccessfully, until Auntie Allie told her to give it back.

Why does Sarah have Down's syndrome?

16. In a Class of Her Own

It is useless to combat idiocy. In order to establish intellectual
activity, it would be necessary to change the conformations of
the organs which are beyond reach of all modifications.

(Medical dictionary, 1838)

Like most children, Sarah often interrupts activities or conversation with constant questioning. Every suggested task or
prospective plan is met by a 'Why?' It reminded me of the boy,
who comes home from school and asks his dad a series of
questions:

Boy: Dad, why is the sky blue?
Dad: Um ... well ... actually, I'm not sure, son.
Boy: And what about the sea?
Dad: Oh ... er ... well ... because it's, er ... oh, I don't know.
Boy: And why does thunder make a noise?
Dad: Oh, I really have no idea.
Boy: Dad, you don't mind me asking all these questions, do
       you?
Dad: No, of course not, son. I mean, how else are you going to learn
       anything?

The subject of 'learning' and education has now become a
national obsession for parents, who are desperate to achieve all
that they can for their children at what seems to be an extraordinarily early age. Discussion by the chattering classes about the
other type of classes is based on the notion of subjective league

tables, SATS results and the open rivalry between local primary and even nursery schools.

As Sarah Boston writes in *Too Deep for Tears*, 'For almost all parents, the way forward to wider social acceptance of their child is through education. Only this kind of contact they feel can break down the barriers of ignorance and fear.' It is probably for this reason that the education of children with special needs is an issue that causes more dissatisfaction, frustration and argument than almost anything else. There are always stories in the Press and on the news about families battling with local education authorities to provide adequate education for their offspring. In order to understand the frustration experienced by parents, we need to look back at the historical sequence of events.

Probably the first time that children with learning difficulties were even considered to be worth bothering about was in 1839, when a French educator and social reformer, Edouard Seguin, opened the first school in the history of special education. Initially housed in a hospital, impressive results were attained and he was then provided with school premises to continue his work. He proved that children previously considered as ineducable could actually be taught literacy and numeracy using methods specifically geared to individual needs.

Seguin designed apparatus to improve physical co-ordination and develop fine motor control and introduced music therapy. Various activities such as carpentry, handicrafts and agriculture were used to bring about fundamental changes in behaviour, skills and the quality of life of his pupils. His methods were so successful that they became a model for the now world famous Montessori schools.

In England and Wales, categories of pupils requiring special educational treatment were first defined in 1959 in the Handicapped Pupils and Special Schools Regulations. Twelve years later, the law was altered to establish a new category of schools which brought all children – regardless of the degree of handicap

– under the care and jurisdiction of Ministry of Education. No child could be deemed ineducable. The responsibility of educating children with learning difficulties transferred from the Department of Health to the Department of Education – a symbolically important move.

A Royal Commission chaired by Baroness Warnock then researched the host of existing special schooling that had come into existence since the 1944 Education Act. The emphasis from then on was to integrate as many children as possible into mainstream schools and devising special programmes to facilitate individual development in a variety of socially relevant skills.

The Education Act of 1981 stated that a child has 'special needs' if he or she has a 'learning difficulty' and provided a number of important safeguards for the child, the parents and local education authorities.

As ever, the practice has not measured up to the theory and there have been many problems in this particular area. Local authorities have been cutting back on spending since the mid-1970s and financial constraints have prevented many councils from discharging their responsibilities. They argue that they cannot afford the cost of supporting disabled children in mainstream schools and continue to implement a policy of segregation. The local authorities have invested in special schools and do not want to see the investment wasted. The use of Assessment and Statement procedures defined in the 1981 Act to assess each child's educational needs are still woefully underused and there are continuing budgetary disputes between education and health authorities about the funding for such vital services as speech therapy.

The government's 1997 Green Paper, 'Excellence for All Children – Meeting Special Educational Needs', further undermines the future use of statementing, as it is clear that the number of future statements is to be reduced. There is little emphasis in the Green Paper on the individual child's right to have his or her special needs met by special educational provision. Some of its aims, such as increasing the proportion of children with special needs in mainstream schools, are laudable, but it is difficult to see how effective this will be without the mechanisms to enforce local authorities to fulfil their responsibilities.

Education can supposedly remain a full-time option until the age of nineteen, as a number of Further Education colleges run life skills and other courses. There are sheltered workshops and adult training centres, but they are not always the most inspiring of places and do not necessarily provide the 'training' that is suitable to adults with Down's syndrome.

In the summer of 1995 Mared Jones, a sixteen-year-old schoolgirl from Clwyd in North Wales, achieved eight GCSE passes. Not that unusual, one might think, except for the fact that at the time of her birth, Mared's parents were told that she couldn't hope for more than a 'limited' life and that they 'must not expect O levels or anything like that'.

Mared, who has Down's syndrome, was fortunate to have articulate, tirelessly dedicated parents who were determined to seek the best for their child and battled for her education to continue in a mainstream secondary school. Mared confounded 'experts' who stated that her level of achievement would soon level off as she aspired to greater things. It also appears that her parents have not pushed her beyond her capabilities and have not put emphasis just on academic achievement. 'We just wanted her to be educated alongside the friends she played with at home, so, she aspired to normality, not the abnormality she would have found in a special school. She has had to fend for herself with her peers and become streetwise. Integration and independence is far more important than academic achievements.'

Sue Buckley, Professor of Psychology of Development Disability at the Down's Syndrome Educational Trust, states, 'Integration is crucial to children's intellectual as well as personal development as language cannot grow if they only interact with others who have similar problems.'

Of course not every child with Down's syndrome can be another Mared Jones and there is no doubt that she is the exception, but it is also true that all children must be given the opportunity to emulate her success. For some parents, 'special schooling' is a viable option for their children. There is, after all, a feeling of safety and security and a sense of protection from the outside world. I would never reject the idea of a special school for Sarah if in the future she simply could not cope with the pressures of a mainstream school and she was unhappy. But parents of special needs children must have the opportunity to make that decision and the selection must be based on viable alternatives. The idea of 'parent choice' has proved to be a nonsense in most cases and the situation remains even more of a myth for parents of children with special needs, who are often afforded no choice at all.

The 1993 Education Act introduced a system of independent special educational needs tribunals with legally qualified chairpersons who could make binding decisions on local education authorities in disputes over mainstream schooling. The appointment of these impartial arbiters has, on the whole, been helpful and has provided parents with the opportunity to challenge the philosophy of education authorities. The achievements of some parents in this matter does, however, seem to be based on a knowledge of the system and the necessity to be well informed or supported throughout the process. The general experience of most parents has not been very successful. I have to say, however, that so far we have been very fortunate and have had only positive experiences in terms of Sarah's schooling.

Sarah's more formal education started at age three with her attendance at Hilltop playgroup which Daniel had also attended two years previously. Daniel had spent a very happy pre-nursery year there and we were anxious for Sarah also to attend. But, of course, with Sarah we thought that there might be problems. Doubts about Sarah's abilities, lack of potty training and the stigma of the syndrome engulfed us. Although we knew the staff well and they had met Sarah through Daniel's attendance, we were unsure how they would react to having a child with special needs in what was a very cosy set-up.

As with our childminding experience, we needn't have worried. Provision had actually just been made for a place for a child with special needs and so Sarah was accepted without any problem. We were also told that even if this hadn't been the case, Sarah would have been admitted in the same way as any other child. The staff were more than happy to have her, even though it meant them having to change her nappies and – because she could only communicate verbally with the odd word – they learned some of the basic Makaton signs from a speech therapist.

This was the integration that we so desired and as one of the play leaders, Ruth Meyers, says, 'The other children just saw Sarah for who she was – a friendly little girl who participated in all the activities with great enthusiasm. They were unaware of her condition and the label Down's syndrome was irrelevant.'

Sarah was thus the first child with special needs to attend Hilltop, but since then there have been a number of others and the playgroup continues to show a true commitment to providing a resource that is very special – in all senses of the word.

At the time of Sarah's birth, most of the usual family concerns were kept in abeyance as far as possible. However, despite all the drama, Daniel's future education did need to be addressed. He would be nursery age the following year and we needed to put his name down for prospective schools.

Local opinion was unambiguous. We were just outside the catchment area for the nearest and most popular primary school, which was set in greenery on the edge of our nearest park. Despite the urban environment, it had an almost villagey air about it. We likened it to the Thrush Green books and one almost expected the headmistress to be another Miss Clare. The school had an excellent reputation and even at this early stage of the educational merry-go-round, we had missed our ride. Our school was to be the one that people took one look at and shuddered – a crumbling Victorian fright set on a busy main road that exuded more lead than Dodge City.

Our special needs health visitor had advised us that Sarah would be better off in the former school as the classes were smaller and her level of concentration might not be terribly acute. We thus decided to try and obtain a place at 'Fairacre' for Daniel as the older sibling. Armed with this information and feeling that at least we were trying to do something positive for Sarah, Allie went to visit the school with the eight-week-old Sarah, nestling cosily in her baby sling.

Allie was totally unprepared for the attitude of the head teacher, who was no Dolly Clare. She was extremely disdainful and made Allie feel smaller than the Reception year pupils.

'We've already got the Deaf Unit here, we can't have any more of these kinds of children ... Our classes aren't smaller than Bounds Green school – these special needs health visitors don't know what they're talking about ... You live outside our catchment area anyway, so I couldn't possibly consider your request whatever the circumstances.'

Allie arrived home in tears, hurt and upset. Oblivious to her vulnerability, the head's insensitivity had further fuelled Allie's anxieties. It seemed that not only was our plan not going to work out, but more significantly, the battle for mainstream education that we had been warned about was already starting. Allie felt that she would never have the strength to face the struggles ahead when at that stage just surviving the day was difficult enough.

In fact this encounter has been the most negative of all our contact with the local education department to date. Although we have a very long way to go, our experiences so far have shown us that there are many professionals who are prepared to give pupils like Sarah a chance to participate in the mainstream experience.

A little under a year before Sarah was due to begin at the nursery, contact from an educational psychologist heralded the beginning of the statementing process. This document or 'statement' (prepared by all involved with Sarah) was to detail all her needs and the help she should receive in order to meet these needs whilst at school. Our educational psychologist was clearly very taken with Sarah, who revelled in the delights of showing off her abilities to a rapt audience. This, together with the psychologist's own beliefs about the value of mainstream education and the local authority's policy, made for an unexpectedly smooth passage through the potential horrors of the early stages of the procedure. The psychologist was in fact so enthusiastic that she told Allie she would like to see Sarah be able to progress to the nearest single sex secondary school. As much as Allie was delighted at the thought of Sarah being able to achieve this, she admitted that she also felt highly anxious at this prospect. Having attended a similar school herself and remembering painfully how much emphasis was placed on 'brains and beauty', she realized we needed to take each year on its own merits and that to leap ahead in this way was extremely daunting. Perhaps we should just concentrate on Sarah playing in the home corner and enjoying story time first.

In the meantime, Daniel had started to attend Bounds Green School and its poor appearance and situation took on much less importance when compared to the enthusiasm and commitment of the teaching staff and the atmosphere within the school. He had enjoyed a very happy year in its nursery class and following the statementing process, Sarah followed suit two years later.

The nursery class staff treated Sarah's arrival with ebullience and expertise. Aided and abetted by the ubiquitous Sarah Stubbs,

Sarah's progress was monitored by regular reviews, planning meetings attended by teachers, speech therapists, a special educational needs co-ordinating officer and input from an educational psychologist. With so many professionals involved, there is an even greater need for co-operation and communication and we have been fortunate to have benefited from each of them.

During this period we were using Makaton sign language and the staff and pupils took to it with great gusto. Within a few months, the pupils had learned a few basic signs and a special Makaton assembly had taken place to present to the rest of the school. I would arrive in the morning with Sarah to be greeted by various toddlers using the Makaton for 'Good morning'. This sign – a thumbs up followed by moving the hand across the chest – was used so much by all the children in greeting each other and the staff, that one teacher remarked that she spent so much time using this particular sign that she felt 'like a priest!'

Towards the end of her year in the nursery class at Bounds Green Infant School, discussions started to take place about Sarah's ability to continue into the next stage of the primary school. We had assumed that Sarah would automatically proceed, but the staff were extremely diligent in discussing whether Sarah was ready to move on and to prepare for any possible pitfalls. It was felt by all, however, that she would cope with the reception year and could move on to the team known as the Beeches.

The system of teaching in the primary school is that of vertical grouping. At first I thought that this meant there wasn't enough money for chairs, but it transpired that this was a method of teaching three consecutive years in one class team. The ages of the children in the team can thus range from four to seven, but within the team they are divided into 'olders', 'middles' and 'youngers'. There are needless to say three teachers to cope with this arrangement!

There was also full discussion about whether Sarah should join Daniel in the same team and whether anything might be gained by keeping them apart for the school day. We had some concerns that Daniel might be made to feel too responsible in looking after his younger sister, but we mainly thought that if they were together, it would give Sarah some continuity and security, as she already knew the teachers, pupils and classroom. When we suggested to Daniel that Sarah might be in another team to him, he was horrified and became quite upset. We thus decided that this arrangement would benefit both children and it was agreed that Sarah would join Daniel in the Beeches – so it was once more unto the Beeches, dear friends, once more.

Sarah settled in as easily as she had done in the nursery and soon became involved in the team's routines. Every morning the register would be taken and being an extremely enlightened school with pupils from a wide variety of cultural and ethnic backgrounds, the children are encouraged – rather than just saying 'here' – to state their presence with a salutation in any language they choose. Daniel, who was very proud of the fact that his maternal grandfather was born in Prague, had decided to adopt the Czech greeting of 'Good day' – *Dobrý den*.

One morning, a fortnight after Sarah had started at infant school, Allie decided to see how Sarah would respond to this procedure. She hid in the corridor whilst the register was taken and awaited for the name of 'Sarah Merriman'. Would Sarah realize what this was about? Would she be aware enough to reply? Would she do this quickly enough and if so how could she cope with her limited language?

As her name was read out, Sarah, with great concentration and perfect accent, responded with . . . '*Dobrý Den!*' Of course Sarah was only copying her brother, but it was very gratifying to know that Sarah – a child with special educational needs – was well on her way to being bilingual in English and Czech!

Every step of the way is encouraged by the school staff and each of Sarah's achievements is greeted with great enthusiasm and real pleasure by the teachers. Despite all the extreme pressures of an urban London school, Sarah's individual needs continue to be explored positively and creatively.

Our speech therapist, Marie Watson, who is very experienced in observing children in their school settings, was extremely complimentary in her view of Bounds Green School. She said that to use the method of vertical grouping with such a wide ranging group of children and in such a large classroom would usually create chaos. However, in this instance, she felt that due to the expertise of the staff there was 'an organised and happy environment that seemed to create a positive self image for the children'. Within this background, she discovered Sarah to be 'integrating well, to be very intelligible, focused and self contained'.

The other vital aspect of Sarah's continuing education was having the continuity of Sarah Stubbs who remained as her special needs assistant. Although this had been her first job in this capacity, Sarah Stubbs had had quite a lot of experience in the school lunchtime supervision of a boy with Down's syndrome and showed herself to be utterly dedicated and committed. She is also extremely imaginative in devising programmes and creating new interests for Sarah and has even enlisted the support of her son Gary, who is a talented artist and created a series of cartoons to help with Sarah's learning. The two Sarahs warmed to each other instantly and they have a very special rapport.

Sarah Stubbs's other charge is Stephen, who has spina bifida and uses a wheelchair to get around. In order to introduce Sarah and Stephen to the school, the staff arranged another special assembly. The idea was to ensure that they were not patronized but that the situation was explained and clarified with the minimum of fuss. The staff talked about Sarah and Stephen, who were still in the nursery class, and explained that they had special needs. Daniel and Stephen's sister, Rebecca, were invited to answer questions from the other pupils.

Allie was a little concerned that Daniel might feel embarrassed by this attention, but in fact he felt 'very proud' that he was able to talk about his sister coming to join the team. He was, however, slightly disappointed that there did not seem to be much interest in Sarah – the children's queries were mainly directed towards Stephen (perhaps because his needs were more visible). One boy asked, 'If he's in a wheelchair, how's he going to eat his lunch properly?' You see, you can always rely on a six-year-old to cut through the nonsense and get to the heart of the matter!

Yet another Sarah has been instrumental in helping the educational process. Sarah Duffen is a young woman in her twenties who has Down's syndrome. When she was very young her father, Leslie, taught her to read using an approach which tackled conceptual problems, such as associating an object with a picture of it. Following contact with Sue Buckley, then a lecturer at Portsmouth Polytechnic (now University of Portsmouth), it was proved that it was possible to teach a substantial sight vocabulary to children with Down's syndrome before they started school. This led to the founding of the Down Syndrome Educational Trust.

This very same method was used by the school when it became apparent that Sarah was not picking up the reading skills as easily as her peers. Our extremely efficient and dedicated special educational needs co-ordinator, Lucy Rodgers, approached the Trust and, employing their material, introduced Sarah to a new reading regime.

Research has shown that 80 per cent of children with Down's syndrome are able to learn to read and with this literacy, speech will improve. Sue Buckley found that most children with Down's syndrome can learn and remember whole words just as easily as other children of their age. However, the amount of vocabulary will be smaller so any reading must be fitted into the stage of language development.

Using this principle, words on flashcards were chosen from Sarah's most familiar vocabulary. The first words were names of family members and were initially matched with photographs to familiarize herself with their meaning. Once she was acquainted with the text, the photographs were withdrawn. In this way, with a very gradual introduction of new words, Sarah has learned to read a fair number of single names and everyday objects. We hope that once Sarah finds reading easier, new words not yet in her vocabulary can be introduced and grammar and sentence structure could then be taught to improve her speech.

Sarah loves reading and likes to be surrounded by books. She also likes to pretend she's a teacher reading to her class and relates the story as she turns the page. Often the story bears little relation to what is written, but at the present time her exposition of fantasy is more advanced than her reading skills. Although I am obviously keen for these to improve, I am delighted that her imagination is so fertile.

Being taught how to use a computer is now in the National Curriculum and Sarah has access to one in her classroom. There is no doubt that this will be of benefit to her in a number of ways. Children with Down's syndrome are much better at learning from visual stimuli than auditory stimuli and if there are some language problems, they are able to express themselves more easily by the written word. If Sarah's handwriting is as illegible as mine, she will benefit by being able to type and should be able to overcome any difficulties of fine motor control by using a keyboard. Certain adaptations such as a large mouse or simplified keyboard can also help. Touch screens and windows can encourage exploration and develop hand–eye co-ordination. Most importantly, the use of computers can help Sarah learn numeracy and literacy whilst having fun!

Perhaps the only slight difference of opinion with the school resulted in a well-intentioned, but ultimately erroneous idea to introduce a doll which had Down's syndrome features. It was suggested that this doll may be useful to reflect Sarah's identity in the same way it was common to have dolls representing various ethnic groups. The doll was ordered on a sale or return basis and Allie was asked to look at it and give her opinion. There seemed to be two major problems with the concept.

First, the doll's rather adult looking features coupled with her various Down's syndrome features gave her a distinctly odd appearance. Were the doll's somewhat slanting eyes with their epicanthic folds, her anatomically correct palmic creases and gaps between the first two toes really of relevance to Sarah's young schoolmates? After all, Sarah had so far been accepted as she was and her 'different' physical features seemed to blend into the wide variation of physiognomy reflected in the school.

Second, since Sarah was the sole child with Down's syndrome in the school, the doll was certain to become a 'Sarah doll' and hence a caricature of her. Unless one was going to have a doll representing every child, this could only serve to introduce an unnecessary negative image of Sarah.

Fortunately, there was no difficulty in making our thoughts known and it was decided that the introduction of the doll would not be beneficial to Sarah or the other children in their understanding of her and so the whole idea was dropped.

Despite many good experiences and the established trust with the education professionals, there is still a certain nervousness before each school review, which is attended by all the involved disciplines. We worry that some negative aspects of Sarah's school life will emerge that we have not been aware of and that some new unexplored problems will appear. However, this has not yet been the case and the only doubts are raised by ourselves, who sometimes cannot believe how well Sarah is doing and need constant reassurance about her abilities.

There is the danger of us all spending every waking hour trying to push our children with Down's syndrome as far as we possibly can academically and at the expense of other attributes. Human achievement should not just be measured in terms of exam success, but also by broader life skills and we feel the school has addressed this concept at all levels creating an environment for Sarah where she is blossoming.

Sarah has made a great deal of progress over the year. She settled well into school and thoroughly enjoys it. She is a personable member of the team and has made close friends with children. No doubt her reading and fine motor skills are areas where she has made much progress and these will be further expanded in Year One. She is increasingly confident and I hope this confidence will lead her to try some areas of the curriculum with greater independence.

Anita Brady (Class Teacher, Bounds Green School)

17. Am I My Sister's Keeper?

Govern a family as you would cook a small fish – very gently.
(Chinese proverb)

We once asked Daniel if he minded that Sarah had Down's syndrome. 'No,' he replied, 'because I love her.' He also once said that he was glad he didn't have Down's syndrome because 'I might be like Sarah and she can be really annoying.'

This just goes to prove that the relationship between them is essentially of a very normal sibling nature. And yet, of course, in many ways it's not. Poor Daniel is probably sick to death of hearing about Down's syndrome. The topic has dominated our lives since Sarah's birth. In addition to all the extra attention she has received from various health and education professionals as well as friends and relatives, there have also been radio shows, television interviews, newspaper articles and now this book about her.

Although Daniel was only just over two years old when Sarah was born and couldn't possibly comprehend the full implications of her birth, he must have been aware of the tension, sadness and confusion that pervaded our household. As the months went by, we tried to explain the differences between Sarah and other children in simple terms. I suppose the fact that Daniel was so young gave us the freedom to explain a little at a time and to judge how much he could understand at each stage of Sarah's development. We didn't have the dilemma of some families, who have older children and may not know quite how much to share or indeed what negative thoughts about people with Down's syndrome the siblings may already have.

One hears of the 'conspiracy of silence' when older siblings are kept in the dark about their parents' true feelings which can exacerbate any guilt or existing worries and make them feel excluded. Involving the older siblings too much can place pressure on children who will automatically feel responsible for their disabled sibling. We know of one man who blames his alcoholism and depression on the expectation of having to care in the future for his younger sister who has Down's syndrome.

From the time that Daniel could first comprehend what it meant to have a sister with Down's syndrome he has been aware of her disability and in fact he used to play games with her that involved the extra help that she was receiving. Instead of playing doctors and nurses, they would sometimes take on other roles: 'I'll be Sarah and you be the physiotherapist.' 'You be Sarah and I'll be the speech therapist.' Of course we did encourage this. Not only would it mean that they bonded nicely as brother and sister, spent hours entertaining each other, but it also saved us a fortune in professional fees!

All siblings have feelings of jealousy and rivalry. We all know how much more these feelings can be brought to the fore by the arrival of a new baby, who will inevitably need a lot of attention. But when a new baby like Sarah joins the family, the effect on existing siblings can be quite profound. The necessity of being open and honest with Daniel has to be counterbalanced with the fact that he must not be overburdened by what can easily become a family obsession.

We have also been vigilant in trying not to use the word 'special' in describing Sarah. Although Daniel is aware of her 'special needs', to hear his sister being constantly labelled as special is enough to make him tear his hair out – or even hers.

From a very early age, Daniel has found Sarah's presence very comforting. At the end of his day at nursery when he was met by Allie and Sarah, he used to go straight up to Sarah and stroke her face for a few minutes before he would consider leaving the school premises. He is incredibly affectionate towards her and is also very proud – always being the first to praise any achievement or new milestone.

On the whole, Daniel is very patient with Sarah. There are things, however, that test his resolve. Sarah is generally slower at expressing herself and is physically less adept. She sometimes takes ages to come down the stairs when we are all waiting to go out and also wants to check each detail of where we are going before she will consider getting ready. When tired or concentrating on a book or a drawing, she has an inclination to make a long, loud droning sound, which can be extremely irritating. Once we assured ourselves that this was not a Buddhist mantra and that we were not preventing her from attaining a higher form of spiritual being, we tried – unsuccessfully – to put an end to this dreadful noise.

Daniel can also find it annoying that Sarah can be quite repetitive – she tends to ask the same question over and over and won't stop until she gets an answer each time. She also likes to know what she and the rest of the family are doing on a particular morning or afternoon and goes through our plans quite obsessively a number of times. We can still occasionally find it difficult to understand the odd word that she is trying to articulate and so Daniel is summoned as her own personal interpreter.

In Cliff Cunningham's book, *Down's Syndrome: An Introduction for Parents*, it is stated that 'There is no evidence that having a [Down's syndrome] child in the family automatically produces ill-effects in the other children . . . in fact there is evidence that many families gain from the experience.'

I talked about this with Alice O'Neill, a senior nurse, whose sister Mary is thirty-five and has Down's syndrome. The O'Neill family are from a small town in Northern Ireland, where there is a very high incidence of Down's syndrome and – maybe this is not a coincidence – where Mary was always accepted for who she was, not what she was.

Alice and Mary have two other sisters and their mother, an obstetrician, died when the girls were still at school. Their father ran a hotel in County Down and apart from support from an uncle, brought up the four girls on his own. The hotel life provided some security for Mary, but placed restrictions on what she could do and where she could go. There were concerns that Mary might bother the residents and she had been known to climb out of her bedroom window at night and be found throwing tantrums in the hotel bar if she wasn't given her favourite drink. (Probably an experience not completely unknown to hoteliers across the world.) Alice was sometimes embarrassed by this and other demanding behaviour – particularly in the local sweetshop! – but doesn't remember any taunting or teasing from friends. This was probably due to the fact that everyone knew each other and although no one denied that Mary was 'different', she was also just one of the O'Neill sisters. Comparisons between the four sisters were seldom made apart from the fact that, in later years, Mary's table manners set the family standards in exemplary mealtime etiquette!

Alice's main recollection of Mary when she was young was that she was 'small and sweet' and she talks of Mary's 'soulfulness and pure innocence', 'sense of fun' and 'poise' with deep affection. Alice does indeed feel that she grew up with a much greater understanding of the notion of disability and now feels a great interest in and affinity with people with Down's syndrome. This is certainly true of Daniel who at the age of seven can spot someone who has Down's syndrome very quickly and wants to know all about them.

Although Mary is now cared for in a hospital, having not been able to cope in a residential unit, the sisters all wish to be involved in decisions about Mary's future and feel a collective responsibility for her – not out of duty, but from choice.

The general feeling of parents is that their other children are not adversely affected of having a sibling with Down's syndrome. It appears, in fact, that the experience of having a sibling with a disability can make them more mature, sensitive and considerate. This has been borne out so far and Daniel's patience has manifested itself in his relationship with a number of toddlers with whom he seems to be particularly popular. Daniel is no angel and has his moments like any other young boy, but in terms of his relationship with Sarah, he does seem to understand her better than anybody and is generally quite tolerant of her ways and foibles. Of course, their relationship is by no means one sided – it is quite symbiotic. Research has shown that a sibling can enhance the social environment of a disabled child and thus have a positive effect on his or her progress. I'm quite sure that this is true for Sarah and in any case, she adores her big brother. They start every day with a huge hug and then wish each other 'Good morning', asking each other if they slept well.

As a person without brothers and sisters, I have never been really aware of the advantages of such close relatives. I suppose they have their uses. I realize that one learns family traditions, domestic rules and social skills from older siblings as well as being able to copy their homework. Younger sisters can provide useful introductions to girls and someone to blame for misdemeanours, but it is true that one's sibling relationship could be the most stable or indeed only stable relationship in your life. Siblings also generally spend more time with each other than they do with their parents.

There is a very interesting book written in 1986 by Peter and Roger Moody entitled *Half Left*. Peter has Down's syndrome and his younger brother Roger is a journalist. It is a quirky and irreverent account of their relationship over many years and describes Peter's life in a very unusual style. It is, however, not just the story of Peter's life – he was born in 1938 – but a description of what it was like to have a 'mental handicap' (as it was termed) throughout five decades and gives a personal and historical view.

Roger describes how, as a young boy, the differences in Peter's character fascinated him and how he found some of Peter's behaviour 'unfathomable'. When friends came around, he spent much time in trying to 'explain Peter away'. His overriding feeling was, however, that Peter was his brother and that he had to know why he was his brother and what it meant to him. When the brothers grew into adulthood, Roger began to question the real meaning of normality. 'The book is written not to show that Peter is exceptional, let alone to show his brother's unique qualities in dealing with him. The relationship we have can be forged by anyone . . . most of this book casts strong doubt on the conventional wisdom that it's Roger who is normal and Peter who isn't.'

There are, of course, great difficulties in any sibling relationship and there are obvious and not so obvious traps to fall into. There is a tendency to let Sarah get away with things in the pretence that it is not that her behaviour is bad, but that it's because she doesn't understand what she is being told. The possible idea that his sister is not a 'naughty girl', but she is a 'Down's girl' and therefore not totally responsible for her behaviour, cuts no ice with Daniel, who is quicker than us to spot any possible play acting!

Daniel also points out that we are much quicker to punish him than Sarah and I'm afraid that this is true on occasions. He maintains that we are much more likely to give her a second or even third chance to improve her behaviour whilst he is only given one opportunity. The old parental threat of buying time by saying, 'You'll be in big trouble if you don't come here by the time I've counted to three' and slowing down to include, 'two

... two and a quarter ... two and three quarters ...' is quite common, but dwelling on two and sixty-three sixty-fourths to let Sarah off the hook is, I admit, going a bit far. Daniel is not impressed – apart from by my knowledge of fractions.

There is always the temptation to compare your children's achievements at each age or stage of development. Watching old videos of Daniel at different ages can be quite distressing when one realizes the gaps between their levels of attainment. I suppose the difference in abilities of speech is the most upsetting. Daniel could easily construct a short sentence at the age of two, whilst Sarah at the age of five is just beginning to do so.

Daniel is particularly good at art and has won a couple of competitions – he had a drawing published in the *Sesame Street* magazine and a picture of one of the Spurs players won him a replica kit and the honour of being in the official team photograph. Sarah's drawing is, however, much less impressive and she still has difficulty in producing anything recognizable. Of course, it also true that Daniel is already a much better artist than me – I can only draw breath – and so the difference in ability cannot just be attributed to Down's syndrome.

Daniel also likes dancing and is quite good. When he asks whether he or Sarah is a better dancer, we are non-committal. 'You're very good, but then so is Sarah ...' Competitiveness and comparison of sibling accomplishment is a common problem for all parents in their efforts to be fair, but the subtext with Sarah is the fact that she has Down's syndrome and that we must therefore lower our expectations. It is important to praise and celebrate Daniel's achievements, but we must always acknowledge the differences between him and Sarah.

I have been told that sometimes siblings will not admit that they have a brother or sister who has special needs. Not because they may be embarrassed by their disability, but they don't necessarily want to have to explain what is wrong with their family member. One is aware of siblings who are embarrassed at having friends home to play – not the case with Daniel, whose friends seem to be genuinely fond of Sarah and unaware of her 'difference'. She is just like any other younger sister who sometimes gets in the way and can be annoying.

To our knowledge, Sarah has never been bullied and Daniel has never been subjected to teasing about his sister, but it is something that will no doubt happen in the future. We decided to tackle this issue in the pilot episode of *Minor Adjustment* and in this scene, Richard and Sarah Stubbs are summoned to the headmaster's office. Kate, who is aged fifteen, has been involved in 'an incident' at school with a fellow pupil, James Morris. Kate's father Richard is convinced that the incident is of a lascivious nature.

Fade up on headmaster's office where the headmaster Mr Shelley is already talking to the boy's mother, Mrs Morris.

Head: … yes, Mrs Morris, I'm afraid it is getting a bit of a struggle financially. There just aren't enough books to go around.

Mrs Morris: That really is awful, Mr Shelley.

Head: So, I'm afraid we're having to cut down. As one of my English teachers said, 'Next term we'll be reading "A Tale of One City" and "The Merry Wife of Windsor".'

They both laugh.

F/X knock on door.

Head: [calling] Yes?

F/X door opening.

Head: Good afternoon. Do come in. Ah – I see we've got the whole Stubbs family here. This is Mrs Morris.

Mrs Morris: Hello.

Head: And her son, James.

Richard: [aside] So that's him, is it? The father of the child.

Sarah: [whispering] Shut up, Richard!

Head: Please sit down. Thank you all for coming. I wanted to get this matter sorted out as quickly as possible. I'll come straight to the point. James and Kate have been excluded from school following an incident that took place in the playground yesterday.

Richard: [aside] Oh no! Not in the playground!

Head: The one thing that we will not tolerate at this school is any form of physical violence. We take a very poor view of one pupil striking another.

Richard: Kate, did he hit you?

Head: No, Mr Stubbs – I'm afraid it was the other way round. Wasn't it, James?

James: Yes. Look what she did to my eye!

Sarah: Oh my God!

Head: It was Kate that hit James.

Richard: I don't believe it…

James: Neither do I.

Sarah: And how did it happen?

James: Well, she caught me off my guard – I wasn't looking.

Mrs Morris: That's not what Mrs Stubbs meant.

Richard: Kate, why did you hit him?

Kate: Well … I …

Head: Just a minute, Kate. I think we should hear from James.

James: [embarrassed] Do I have to?

Head: Yes, especially as little Amy is here.

Sarah: What's this to do with Amy?

Head: We're waiting, James … what happened?

James: Well, I was in the playground when all of a sudden, Kate belted me.

Kate: What did you expect, after all those things you said about my sister.

Mrs Morris: What things? You haven't told me about this part of it!

James: [sheepishly] No … well … I didn't…

Mrs Morris: … I want the truth, James.

James: I didn't really mean it … I …

Kate: … Yes, you did!

Head:	What exactly did you say to Kate?
Kate:	I'll tell you what he said! He said Amy was a freak, a retard who would have to live in a loony bin when she grew up.
Mrs Morris:	[horrified] Oh no!
Kate:	And that was just part of it.
Sarah:	James, why did you say that?
Kate:	I'll tell you. He's been asking me out for months and I kept saying no. In the end he just got cross and said, 'You're just like your little sister – funny in the head.' I really would be funny in the head if I'd gone out with him.
Head:	Now, that's enough, Kate.
Kate:	So, in the end, I had no alternative but to knock him out.
Richard:	You knocked him out!
Mrs Morris:	I feel awful about this. I'm so ashamed. I don't know what to say.
Head:	Well, no doubt you'll have plenty to say to James later. However, as I've said, I will not tolerate violence of any kind in this school – no matter how commendable it is that Kate should possess such family loyalty.
Richard:	[to himself] And quite a good right hook…
Head:	… But in spite of the extreme provocation she must learn to restrain herself. I'm sure you agree, Mr and Mrs Stubbs?
Sarah:	Yes, of course.
Head:	Mr Stubbs?
Richard:	[insincerely] Oh … er … yes. Shocking. Terrible. Absolutely disgraceful.
Head:	And as for you, James, I trust that you are ashamed of your behaviour. I don't propose to take this matter any further and you will both return to school on Monday – having had the weekend to cool down. Now, I suggest you apologise to each other.
Kate:	[reluctantly] Sorry.
James:	Sorry.
Head:	Now, I'd like you to shake hands.

James: You must be joking – she'll probably break my arm.

Mrs Morris: [sharply] James!

James: Oh … all right then.

Fade down

When Daniel reaches the same age as his fictitious sister Kate, he will no doubt be more aware of the role he might have to play in the future and will – no matter what we say – believe he is responsible for Sarah.

There is a man with Down's syndrome living nearby, who used to come to Daniel's school with his carer. Daniel, who was then aged four and was already quick to recognize a person with Down's syndrome, asked Allie all about him and why he had a carer to look after him. Allie turned the question back on Daniel and asked him what he thought. Daniel said, 'It's because the man doesn't know what to do.' After thinking about this he added, 'But Sarah already knows what to do.' Allie replied that although Sarah was doing very well, she might still need some help when she reached the same age as this man, and that he shouldn't worry because 'we'll make sure you won't have to help her – there'll be other people to do it if she needs it'. Daniel was quite put out and said simply, 'But, Mummy, I want to.'

Our aim is for Daniel to grow up feeling that he has a choice about how much he wishes to be involved in caring for Sarah. Of course we would be delighted if he wants to play a part in her well-being but he must never feel that there is an expectation. We do not want Daniel to undertake the parental role. It is important that he must not be made to feel resentful towards Sarah by having to act and feel like an adult whilst he is still growing up. One of Allie's reasons for wanting a third child – although by no means the principal one – was that any such feelings of responsibility could be shared and not just experienced by Daniel alone. Of course if there's one thing that this whole experience has taught us it is to be prepared for anything. We cannot predict the future. Although one hopes that Sarah's two brothers, Daniel and Joel, will be happy, successful and rich they actually may not turn out to be the Coen brothers of the new millennium. Who knows – they may end up being a couple of hopeless dweebs and need Sarah to look after them. Although of course, if anyone is going to be a burden on the children, I have first shout.

Joel's subsequent arrival and place in the family is, of course, another story . . . or at least another chapter. In the meantime I think it's only fair that Daniel has his own say.

I like Sarah not just because she's my sister, but because she's sweet, she has a sense of humour and she comes up to me and says, 'Please can you cuddle me.' She can talk a lot now – maybe a bit too much sometimes. In the Infants we were in the same class team but now I'm going to the Juniors and I'm going to miss her.

Sarah is very popular and she has a lot of friends like Thomas, Ellen, Ramzey, India, Yassie, Eliza, Sara and Ella. Sarah loves inviting people round to our house and playing and she really likes playing with Joel. She calls him 'Joely, my baby brother'.

Sarah likes dancing to Michael Jackson and the Spice Girls. If she was a Spice Girl, I think she would be 'Spaghetti Spice' as she likes eating pasta. She also likes eating crisps and anything else she can find in the house.

She quite likes football and like me, she supports Spurs. I'd like to take her to a match, but I think she'd be frightened by the noise of the crowd. She was jealous when I won a competition and was in the team photograph with all the players, but I got David Ginola's autograph for her and she was pleased.

I was pleased when she was in the radio show because then I was jealous of her.

Once when I was in the bath, I remember telling Mummy and Daddy that I was glad I didn't have Down's syndrome because it's difficult for Sarah to learn things. Now I think if Sarah didn't have Down's syndrome, she wouldn't be Sarah and I love her just as she is. I don't want Sarah to have plastic surgery like some children with Down's syndrome because I don't want her to be a different girl.

I love Sarah and I always will.

18. And Yet Another Production

Fade up

F/X Italian restaurant with opera music in background.

Richard: How long is it since we've been here?

Sarah: Oh, I don't know – it must be at least a year.

Richard: They're still playing the same music.

Sarah: Yes.

Richard: And the decor is also much the same, although I think there's one more Chianti bottle hanging from the ceiling.

Sarah: [sharply] Richard.

Richard: And the menu hasn't changed. Prices are up of course.

Sarah: There's probably not much more we can say about Luigi's, is there? So, can we start talking properly now?

Richard: Oh, do we have to?

Sarah: You know we do. You promised.

Richard: All right, all right.

Sarah: Go on then.

Richard: Oh no, that's not fair – you start.

Sarah: Okay. [pause] Well, you know how strongly I feel about this. And these feelings are obviously not going to go away.

Richard: I was afraid of that.

Sarah: I really can't wait any longer – I'll soon be too old.

Richard: That's exactly my point. I feel too old to start again.

Sarah: Oh don't be ridiculous.

Richard: We've been through this so many times – I don't know what else there is to say.

Italian waiter:	[approaching] Have you decided what you would like, madam?
Sarah:	Yes, I'd like a baby.
Waiter:	[pause] Oh. Perhaps you need a little more time.
Sarah:	No, actually, we've had plenty of time to decide.
Waiter:	And what about your husband?
Sarah:	He's not very keen on the idea.
Waiter:	He doesn't want to eat?
Sarah:	No. He doesn't want another baby.
Waiter:	Ohhh. [pause] Signor – you must be crazy! A beautiful lady like this.
Richard:	It's not quite as simple as that.
Waiter:	Oh, but it can be. Believe me I know. You see I have three children.
Richard:	Just because you've got three children, it doesn't mean I have to follow. Two is quite enough for me.
Waiter:	It's not enough.
Richard:	It's plenty.
Sarah:	No, it isn't.
Waiter:	So, why do you not want more, sir?
Richard:	It's a very complicated situation. You see when our second daughter was born we were in a … wait a minute … this is a private matter between me and my wife. I really don't think I want your opinion. Could we just order some food, please?
Sarah:	I suppose my husband's right, but thank you for trying.
Waiter:	My pleasure, signora.
Richard:	Well, I'd like to start with the Antipasti.
Sarah:	So would I.
Waiter:	Ah, you see that's good. You are agreeing already.
Sarah:	And to follow, I'll have the Chicken Cacciotara.
Richard:	Linguini with clam sauce, please.
Waiter:	Yes … very good. And to drink?

Richard:	Is a bottle of Frascati okay, Sarah?
Sarah:	Yes, fine.
Waiter:	Thank you. [going off] And good luck, madam!
Richard:	Well, that's just wonderful, isn't it? Now the waiter knows all about our personal life. He'll probably tell the other waiters and soon the whole restaurant will be talking about us. No doubt the kitchen staff are already taking bets on it.
Sarah:	Well, I think he was very sweet.
Richard:	Yes, but he's also Italian. You know what they're like – they love large families. I knew we should have eaten Chinese tonight – *they* only encourage you to have one child over there.
Sarah:	How are we going to resolve this, Richard?
Richard:	I don't know. I really don't know. This business of the third child has been hanging over us for nearly four years now. There's not a day goes by when you don't mention it in some shape or form.
Sarah:	That's because I'm desperate, Richard.
Richard:	You started talking about this on the day that Amy was born – soon after we knew she had Down's syndrome. If you had your way, you'd have been pregnant again straight away.
Sarah:	I know. And looking back you were right not to agree. Like you said, I hadn't fully accepted Amy and I was just wanting to replace her.
Richard:	And that wouldn't have been fair to her.
Sarah:	But you know that I couldn't love her more.
Richard:	Of course I do. Neither of us could.
Sarah:	But the thing is, I was robbed of the joy that having a baby normally brings. We found it hard to tell people, we didn't want to show her off, our friends didn't know whether to congratulate or commiserate – it was hardly

	a time for celebration. I still want that positive experience that I missed out on.
Richard:	But all of this is what *you* want. What about me? What about Kate and Amy?
Sarah:	I don't want Kate to feel she has the sole responsibility of looking after Amy in the future. And Amy's bound to benefit from the experience of having a younger brother or sister.
Richard:	And I suppose I'm going to benefit from sleepless nights, changing nappies, more expense and worry and an exhausted wife.
Sarah:	But think how happy I'll be.
Richard:	All right. A happy, exhausted wife.
Waiter:	[approaching] Sir, madam. Here you are, *due Antipasti*.
Sarah:	Thank you.
Richard:	Thank you.
Waiter:	Would you like to try the wine, sir?
Richard:	Yes, please.

F/X pouring wine into one glass.

Waiter:	So, how are you two getting on?
Sarah:	Not very well, I'm afraid.
Richard:	[terse] Fine, thank you. [drinking wine] And so is the wine.

F/X pouring second glass of wine.

Sarah:	Thank you.
Waiter:	[going off] I'll put it on ice.
Richard:	I wish I could do the same with this discussion.
Sarah:	Yes, but we can't. You said that we would make a decision by the time Amy was four.
Richard:	But she isn't four yet.
Sarah:	She will be in a few weeks' time.
Richard:	[enthusiastic] Well then we'd better get organised. She'll have to have a party and have you thought about what

	sort of cake she'd like? We'll have to do invitations … games. What about a puppet show?
Sarah:	Richard!
Richard:	All right then − a magician.
Sarah:	That would suit you, wouldn't it? Wave a magic wand and make me disappear.
Richard:	I don't want you to disappear. I'm very happy with you and Kate and Amy. I just don't need anyone else.

Fade down.

Fade up. It is now an hour later.

Waiter:	And this is my eldest … Antonio. He looks just like me. Yes?
Sarah:	Yes, he's very handsome.
Waiter:	Oh … this … is a wonderful picture of Lucia − taken at her first communion.
Sarah:	Oh, doesn't she look sweet, Richard?
Richard:	Yes … yes … she does. Lovely. Now, do you think I could have my espresso please?
Waiter:	And this is Roberto − the *bambino* − he's only six months old. Named after Roberto Baggio, you know.
Sarah:	Oh he's beautiful.
Richard:	Yes … yes … very *belissimo*. And could we also have the bill, please?
Waiter:	Of course sir. I hope I haven't bored you with these photos.
Sarah:	No, of course not.
Waiter:	We were just lucky that the restaurant was rather quiet tonight.
Richard:	[aside] Which is more than we can say for you.
Waiter:	Now the boss has said that as this is a special occasion, you must accept the wine as a gift.
Sarah:	Oh, thank you very much.
Richard:	Wait a minute, this isn't a special occasion.

Sarah:	No, but there might be.
Waiter:	And also there are compliments from the chef.
Richard:	But, aren't we supposed to send our compliments to him?
Waiter:	Ah yes, but he wants to send his compliments to you, signor.
Richard:	What for?
Waiter:	On having such a beautiful wife.
Richard:	Yes – I suppose she is.
Sarah:	Thank you, Richard. [pause] Did he really say that?
Waiter:	Yes. [pause] And he also said that as far as the kitchen staff were concerned, the clever money is on you, signora.

Fade down.

I hadn't realized quite how autobiographical this scene in *Minor Adjustment* was until it was actually broadcast and friends commented on how brave it was to be so public about our own situation. Much of Richard and Sarah's discussion – much abbreviated obviously – had derived from similar talks that Allie and I experienced after Sarah's birth.

Within an hour of Sarah's diagnosis, I was jolted by a conflict so powerful that it was to take a relentless hold on me. My first thought was that I would just have to have another baby. Somehow this would make everything all right again. I must have managed to gain a shred of rationality, however, for my next thought was that there must never be more children. My mission in life was to help and provide for Sarah – further offspring could only diminish this aim.

My mind was so full of all kinds of other jumbled thoughts and feelings that I didn't spend time wondering how this conflict would be resolved.

Before I knew it, I realized that it wasn't a question of choice. It wasn't to be a conscious decision. The need for another child was overwhelming . . . It was almost beyond my control and was to consume all my waking hours.

Allie had started to raise the question of having another child immediately after Sarah's birth. I felt that I just couldn't begin to contemplate another huge decision so soon after such a traumatic event and I refused to discuss the matter, hoping that in time, Allie wouldn't feel so desperate.

I felt that this frantic need for another child was linked to the fact that Allie had not yet been able to show any real affection for Sarah. I feared that if we were to have another child too quickly Allie might preoccupy herself with a new baby and never grow to love Sarah, who would become marginalized and never be fully accepted.

I also felt that because of Sarah's disability, we would need to devote much more time to her than an 'ordinary' child and that I just didn't have the energy to give to another possible member of the family. There was Daniel to consider and I was already aware of the fact that his needs had occasionally been overlooked in all the attention that Sarah had received.

We couldn't really afford another child, I still didn't feel emotionally ready and I really didn't need another child to make my life complete.

Apart from all that I thought it was a great idea.

We had planned to have just two children. If all had gone as expected and Sarah hadn't had Down's syndrome, I believe we would not have seriously considered having a third child.

First, despite the fact that motherhood is the most important part of my life and I couldn't love my children more, I am definitely no earth mother. I am not very

domesticated and I still love to be spontaneous, to go out alone with no feelings of responsibility. Second, I am one of two siblings – as were both my parents. My sister is clear that she does not want any more than her two existing children. It is thus part of our family culture and the average family in Britain consists of 2.2 children. It also makes a kind of logical sense to me. We have two hands – one to hold each child – two eyes and two sides of the brain. Three is far too 'disorganizing' a number for me. But here I was becoming obsessed with a third child even before I had left the labour ward with my second one!

Andy was very clear that my wish for a third child stemmed from the fact that I hadn't accepted Sarah and wanted to replace her. I thus felt trapped in the most dreadful bind. I would somehow have to learn to love Sarah, who at that time felt little more than a physical and emotional burden. She had taken the place of another – the one I had really wanted. This unbearable conflict began to haunt me and yet Andy was refusing to discuss this with me until after Sarah's first birthday. Although I understand the logic of this plan I nonetheless felt 'gagged'.

I did, however, talk about it in depth with dear friends and other people where it felt relevant. I think just being able to voice my thoughts about it in this way helped me to feel closer to the prospect of it actually happening one day.

The desperation I felt at this stage could also have been due to my intense feelings of helplessness. I did soon realize that the birth of a third child would not make any of the difficulties associated with Down's syndrome go away, but I felt strongly that it would at least

help in some way. I had to do whatever I could to rid myself of this sense of powerlessness.

After a couple of months of fruitless 'negotiation', we agreed that we would not talk about another baby for a year – until Sarah's first birthday. We decided to write our thoughts down and then go to a restaurant to discuss our ideas. We thought that if we were in a public place, then I couldn't storm out of the room as I was wont to do at that time and Allie couldn't break down in tears as she was likely to do. It all sounds very controlled and unspontaneous, but it was the only way that we could possibly handle the situation. There was a great deal of strain on our relationship – we seemed to be just about coping with Sarah's existence but now the far-reaching consequences of her birth seemed to be taking more of a toll on us.

Apart from not getting very far in our discussions over the next few months, it also became a very expensive way of not enjoying what was probably very good food! Eventually we abandoned these gastronomic outings, but regular planned discussion continued at home, precipitating great anticipation and nervousness before each occasion.

It seemed somewhat strange to actually arrange a time and date for a discussion with Andy. I dreaded these talks as I was so afraid that Andy wasn't going to change his mind. This anxiety and panic about the prospect of meeting with my own husband, who had also been my best friend for many years, used to strike me as surreal.

This was, however, an unusual situation where no compromise existed. Andy and I had never had differences before when it came to major decisions in our lives and here we were with no middle way. We did consider seeking professional help with this, but agreed as long as

we were still able to keep the channels of communication open, we could continue to try and handle it ourselves. As time went by Andy's original fear of Sarah being marginalized was no longer of relevance. He now knew that my love for Sarah was total and the issues for me were in no way connected to any feelings of replacing her.

I used any possible argument in my desperation to be heard. I remember stepping on very dangerous ground, pleading, and promising that Andy would never have to get up in the night or in the early morning for the baby. I would do everything and he would hardly be aware of the difference in having an extra child. No, I wouldn't be worn out, I would continue to be interested in world affairs, the arts and socializing with friends and I would over-come any physical demands placed on me by a new baby.

'She promised me this, she promised me that, she promised me everything under the sun.' Allie was Nathan to my Adelaide. Allie was offering anything to have another child and I felt so sorry for her. All practicalities were forgotten, all financial considerations abandoned and all domestic realities swept aside by this emotional tidal wave.

Allie had conveniently forgotten that sleep deprivation is a form of torture and now she was offering to undergo further torment single handed. I could see myself becoming more and more tired and pressurized and having no life beyond being responsible for the family. The thought of further domesticity was not blissful and I knew that Allie just wouldn't be able to do all the things she promised. Perhaps, 'I should call a lawyer and sue her.'

But the main issue – if you'll pardon the pun – remained. I just didn't have the same need for enlarging our family. Daniel and Sarah were such wanted children and it was difficult to reconcile the fact that we might be bringing a baby into our family whom I didn't have the same feelings about. It didn't seem fair to any of the rest of us – let alone the 'third child'.

I needed my last experience of pregnancy and childbirth to be as totally joyous as my first time had been – how it was meant to be. My whole identity as a woman and mother had been affected to the core. I knew that I could never feel comfortable again hearing of another woman's pregnancy or news of a newborn baby. I was so sure that by having another experience (and I couldn't let myself consider anything going 'wrong') a healing process would take place. I too could again enjoy the luxury of 'the perfect experience' and lay to rest my bitterness.

Also of great importance was the feeling of 'investment' we perhaps mistakenly make in our children. With two non-disabled children we could keep our expectations completely open. For Sarah, our aspirations had become very high, but nevertheless remained within certain limits. I no longer felt I had problems with this as it related to Sarah, but for our family as a whole I needed to be able to enjoy the privilege of all the hopes and dreams that parents of two 'ordinary' children can afford. After all, there had to be the prospect of the doctor *and* the lawyer!

There were other reasons too. If we did have another child then perhaps Daniel could share any responsibilities as well as other pressures that may be present in being the only non-disabled child. Also, for Sarah, I felt it would be healthy if she was not the 'baby' in the family and would enjoy and benefit from a younger child growing up behind her. With three children, there wouldn't be the 'normal one' and the 'disabled one'. We would just be a family with all sorts of different children.

In the light of all this I felt there was an urgency to get on with the process. We weren't getting any younger, the gap between the new child and Daniel and Sarah was increasing. We were in the swing of having young children. We were used to sleepless nights, being surrounded by nappies and toys. We didn't know how long it might take to conceive and I felt all the risks in pregnancy were gradually increasing.

We did, in fact, go together to see our obstetrician about this latter concern and she surprised me by saying that in fact my fertility was not going to drop significantly until I was forty years old and the only real risk of increasing age related to Down's syndrome, where our risk was one in a hundred anyway. I had been sure her advice would support my point of view, but it contained the message that to delay the decision would not be of any great significance.

The critical fact remained. Andy did not want a third child. I did. I was convinced that a desperation *for* something had to outweigh a desperation *not to have* something. I realize now that this belief was flawed and this was borne solely out of the very yearning I felt.

The only time that I felt able to listen to Andy's point of view was when he talked of how our relationship could suffer as a result of having another child when our feelings in the matter were so opposed. I felt, however, that our relationship could equally suffer if we didn't have another child. My most crucial concern was that Andy would end up resenting the child, although when I asked him about this he told me he was much more likely to resent me.

I realized that this was not exactly the ideal way to bring a new child into the world, but I felt that I could cope with this dichotomy. I also believed that our relationship was strong enough to survive the impact of any resentment that would come my way.

I know Andy felt that this acceptance of the risk to our marriage was an insult. He felt that I didn't value our relationship enough and that a third child meant more to me than having him, Daniel and Sarah. If they all meant as much to me as I said, why would I not be satisfied with our existing family?

I had great difficult explaining how the issues were quite separate. My need to complete our family in this way had no bearing on what I actually felt for each of them. It would be fair to say I became quite obsessed with the prospect of a third child. When I looked at Daniel and Sarah I often imagined another smaller version beside them. I occasionally dared to fantasize a name which went well with 'Daniel' and 'Sarah'. I used to tell Andy of every couple who had increased their family beyond two children – definitely the current fashion. I felt my life was on hold until this decision was made.

People said to me how brave I was to contemplate having another child. I was sure, however, that I would have needed a greater amount of courage to consider living without a third child and deny what was an irresistible urge. Never believe that the desire for a subsequent child can't be as strong as it is for a first child.

People would tell me that Andy would 'come round' in the end. I felt that this idea was based on the idea of Andy's character as being easy-going and malleable. I felt that this was a misguided view as nobody had any idea of the strength of Andy's feelings and resolve about this. This conviction could also, of course, have emerged from their knowledge of my tenacity ... or should I say stubbornness?

For my part I was terribly uncertain as to the likely

outcome and lived from one meeting to the next trying to hang on to any glimmer of hope. I still have a note Andy left for me the day after one such encounter. It contained a list of people who had telephoned and various messages of domestic information. At the end, he had written, 'It will work out . . . I promise!' I decided to interpret this in my favour and at the very least it gave me the reassurance that we were not about to 'go under'.

I had always sworn a terrible oath that I would never end up with three children all under the age of six. Whenever we were out and I would come across such a family, I would point them out to Allie and remind her that this was my nightmare. Poor souls. Look at them . . . desperately trying to enjoy some hideous family event or holiday. Here we were actually discussing this possible scenario, which to me seemed much more frightening than raising a child with Down's syndrome. But Allie wasn't going to be dissuaded – even bribes of world cruises and glorious gifts beyond her wildest dreams didn't, for some reason, distract her from the task in hand.

After an argument, I once left a note for Allie saying, 'It will work out . . . I promise!' I had no idea what I meant by this – it was just a feeble attempt at hoping that everything would work out, but having no earthly clue as to how. Allie took it as a sign that I was finally coming round to her way of thinking and that it was the first stage of a reluctant agreement.

Perhaps she was right.

As time passed and the pressure continued to hang over us, we just weren't making any progress. I couldn't agree to a new baby and yet I couldn't bring myself to say that we could never have another child. Doubts began to appear. Maybe it would be a good idea for Sarah to have a younger sibling to play with. Perhaps it would be fairer to Daniel to have some sibling support.

Allie was becoming more and more unhappy. I knew that if we didn't make a definite decision soon, we would be in real trouble.

Towards the end of Sarah's third year, I decided that Allie was not going to change her mind. If I didn't agree she would be resentful towards me for the rest of her life. She would never forgive me. The only way forward in the circumstances was to have another child. Maybe it would be for the best. I just didn't know.

At the end of May 1995 a pregnancy test confirmed my hopes and although I was obviously delighted, the sobering realities of what lay ahead tinged my excitement. This pregnancy was going to be endured not enjoyed – that experience had been lost for ever.

We were faced with another difficult dilemma. Following Sarah's birth, we were obviously much more aware of what could go 'wrong'. We couldn't love Sarah any more and wouldn't change her in any way, but the thought of having *another* child with a disability was terrifying. We just didn't see how we could cope with another child with Down's syndrome and part of the reason to have another child was to provide some support and security for Daniel and Sarah. Sarah might need our help for the rest of her life. How could we provide a lifetime's commitment of this kind to two children? And how on earth would it affect Daniel?

The chance of us having another child with Down's syndrome was considered to be about one in a hundred. I preferred to be mindlessly optimistic – after all the odds were still very much on our side and it was thus unlikely to happen, but we decided that we couldn't possibly go through the pregnancy and not know what the future held.

I could not bring myself to truly get in touch with what

we would do if I found I was carrying a second child with Down's syndrome. To have a termination in ignorance of the facts must be traumatic enough, but to have an abortion in the light of the fact that we were oblitering an existence because it was like the daughter we have and love deeply would be impossible. A betrayal of Sarah and all those with Down's syndrome.

We decided to have a diagnostic test in the hope of gaining the reassurance we needed, desperately hoping that an impossible choice would not have to be considered should we find we were expecting another child with Down's syndrome or any other disability.

After a few weeks we visited Miss Morgan again and she advised us of all the various tests. I chose an amniocentesis rather than CVS (Chorionic Villas Sampling) as there is less risk of a miscarriage, although the test is performed later and there is a longer wait for the result. Andy wanted to know as soon as possible what we might be facing, but once again I took the decision into my hands and I know he felt pushed aside.

We had to wait till the seventeenth week for the result. As time went by and I felt the baby kicking, I began to regret not opting for the CVS which would have been done at ten weeks. We would now at least know our destiny.

The waiting became intolerable and Andy and I began to quarrel over every little thing. The experience of the amniocentesis was horrific; I realized that I wasn't really prepared for the outcome. At the same time there were the physical aspects. I felt that if I was to move just a millimetre once the needle was inserted, our baby could be stabbed in the eye. I felt an urge to run out of the hospital screaming with the needle still in place. My sense of panic over what was happening was stultifying and it was Andy's reassuring presence that saved us from disaster.

The wait for the result was the longest of my life. One moment I would fear a miscarriage, the next I would be convinced that some sort of abnormality would be detected.

Sixteen days after the test we received a rather ambiguous message on our answering machine to contact the obstetric office the next morning. If it had been good news why hadn't she just said so? Was there something to hide? This led to the most intense feelings of blind terror I have ever experienced – my thoughts were jumbled and I could neither sleep nor do anything productive.

I returned the call first thing the following morning, hardly able to breathe – to discover that the result was 'normal'. I cried with relief. Andy had taken the children to school and I gave him the 'thumbs up' from the window whilst watching him return. Andy got out of the car and lay down in the middle of the road in a gesture of great relief – at least I hoped it was relief and not a suicide attempt. The passing postman seemed quite unconcerned at this unusually rash behaviour and took less notice when I rushed out of the house into the street to throw my arms around Andy.

After these events the pregnancy continued in a relaxed and happy phase for the next few weeks. I then received a telephone call at work from the hospital. 'It's about the Tay-Sachs test, please come to the hospital now for a repeat blood test. Get Andy to come too and we'll get your bloods over to Guy's Hospital in a taxi.'

I rang Guy's Hospital and discovered that the blood had been presented to them incorrectly and this was the reason that the test needed repeating. However, by this time it was hard just to focus on the medical error and I was convinced that the baby had Tay-Sachs disease – children born with it live only for four or five years. This is more prevalent in the Jewish community, but I was told that both parents don't have to be Jewish for Tay-Sachs to occur.

I was terrified as I drove to the hospital. I met Andy there and he was again the voice of reason and helped me feel calmer. He even made me laugh by saying, 'Typical – everything gets blamed on the Jews!'

After a wait of several days, I telephoned Guy's Hospital for the result. We happened to be on holiday and were spending the day on the Isle of Wight. Ironically, I was in close proximity to The Needles when I learned that all was well and we would need no further blood tests. I convinced myself there would be nothing more to be worried by in this pregnancy, although I felt an overall sense of apprehension of what lay ahead.

Joel was born on the first of March 1996 and my overriding emotion was that of pure relief – a relief born out of the fact that he was well and healthy and didn't appear to have any obvious disabilities, which was, after all, one of the main reasons for having another child – but a relief also deriving from the fact that we didn't have to talk about this anymore. Joel was here and there would be no need for any more interminable discussions about 'the third child'. Allie's desperation had been lifted and there was no longer this Sword of Damocles suspended over us. I suppose I should just have taken the clever money into consideration from the very beginning.

All these fears and anxieties were worth it as I watch Joel excitedly playing football in the hallway with his brother and sister. He has no sense yet of the dramas and conflict that his existence elicited and maybe this has actually drawn me even closer to him. He's a great character, very animated, full of fun, mischief and spirit. A real 'Nipper with Attitude'. I know now that having him was the right thing to do and I realize that our family wouldn't be complete without him.

I love Joel as dearly as I do Daniel and Sarah, who are both delighted with their baby brother. Daniel recently asked me, 'Which do you think is better – having Joel as a brother or having him as a son?'

We were convinced that Sarah, in particular, would find it very difficult to cope with a new sibling who would demand much of our time and energy. From the moment she arrived, she was the recipient of much attention and we were sure that she wouldn't take kindly to being out of the limelight on occasions. She overheard us telling a friend that her nose would probably be put out of joint and she soon picked up the idea, saying, 'New baby . . . my nose out the window.'

In fact we were quite wrong and Sarah did not seem to be adversely affected at all. She took to Joel straight away and adores him. Sarah has never been openly jealous of him, loves his company and regularly repeats, 'I love my baby brother,' before adding politely, 'and my big brother.'

19. Paterfamilias Territory

The fathers have eaten a sour grape and the children's teeth are set on edge.

(Jeremiah, 31:29)

A father was talking to his son. 'Well, my boy, it's your birthday and I'm going to give you a very special present.'

'Thanks very much, Dad,' the son replied. 'What is it?'

'It's a cowboy suit, son.'

'That's great, Dad, but . . . um . . . the thing is I'm, er . . . twenty-one now and I've . . . well . . . I've sort of grown out of that kind of thing.'

The father looked slightly hurt, but said, 'Oh, OK. Well, what about a train set or a football?'

'No, Dad. No. You see—'

'Would you like a chemistry set?'

'Well, that's very kind, Dad, but you see . . . well, I've got this girlfriend now and I rather wanted to take her out to dinner tonight. Some cash would be really great.'

'Oh I see. Well, of course, son. You should have said. Here's twenty quid.'

'Thanks very much, Dad. That's great! Bye!'

The young man rushed out, slamming the front door behind him. Ten minutes later, there was a knock at the door and the father opened it to reveal his son, clutching his knee, hair tousled and with tears pouring down his face.

'Oh no! What on earth's the matter?'

'Oh . . . Dad . . .' the son wailed, 'I fell over.'

Children are always your children no matter what age. The responsibility and worry continues until you draw your last breath and was recently highlighted by the case of a twenty-year-old Scottish man who is suing his mother in order to force her to pay for his university education. As Oscar Wilde said, 'Children begin by loving their parents, after a time they judge them, rarely, if ever, do they forgive them.'

The daughter of a friend of ours was chosen as one of the candidates in a mock election at her school. She had to elicit support from her classmates, research local issues and deliver a speech to her class before the election. This was soon after Sarah was born and I was particularly affected by the fact that Sarah would never be in this situation. At the time, I knew she would never be the class heroine and thought then that she may never be able to read and write.

I had this image of Sarah as the class dunce without friends, who wouldn't have a clue what was going on around her. I was very upset and I remember crying uncontrollably. I don't suppose many people have shed tears at the thought of losing a would-be politician from their family, but it was yet another example of Sarah not being able to fulfil *my* expectations.

When this same young woman started university, it also struck me how I would not be able to visit Sarah at college, take her and some of her friends out to lunch and hear all about their academic achievements – or at least which gig they had gone to and how drunk they had got the night before. I felt that I would miss out on an experience that I had always thought about. (There is, of course, always an upside. This same friend's children are now both at college and with all her financial assistance, emotional support and academic guidance, she feels that she has been to secondary school several times and is now participating in her second and third university careers.)

I must always remind myself that Sarah does not exist just to suit my expectations or satisfy my dreams. She is her own person and not someone to be dictated to by an overzealous dad. Perhaps the best recommendation is offered by American president Harry S. Truman who said, 'I have found the best advice to your children is to find out what they want and then advise them to do it.'

Historically, the father's role was seen as primarily social and economic whereas the mother's was essentially biological and nurturing. We now know that this does not have to be the case.

With very few exceptions that do not involve physical strength, women can do almost anything that men can do. Likewise, the notion of childcare which still remains very much in the female domain need not be so bound by traditional roles. The practicalities of childcare hold no mystique – anyone can cuddle, wash, bathe, dress, undress, feed a baby, change a nappy, and then put him or her to bed. When it comes to parenting, there is little that a man cannot do except be pregnant, give birth to a baby and breastfeed. Even in breastfeeding, some men are trying to get in on the act.

I remember some years ago Allie was doing an analytical counselling course and we had dinner with a couple of her colleagues and their partners. We had all just become parents for the first time and inevitably the discussion turned to raising children. Two of the men, precious in the extreme, were bemoaning the fact that they were unable to breastfeed. Biologically bereft, they spoke of the loss that they felt and how this vital bonding process was denied them because they were men.

One of them had discovered a pouch which could be placed around the male pectorals and then filled with milk so that newborn babies could find succour from their pater. The father could then be part of the breastfeeding process and be a proper parent. I was utterly appalled and said something along the lines of, 'You may regard me as somewhat Neanderthal in my approach to parenting, but I would rather stick needles in my eyes than be part of this nonsense.' They were horrified and looked at Allie with great pity. She had obviously made a terrible mistake in marrying a man who had no wish to breastfeed his firstborn.

I think that men who want to breastfeed are confusing the biological reality and have become engaged in a parental power struggle, which is more to do with primacy than fatherhood. At the time of the birth and neonatal period, the mother–child bond is the primary attachment. The father–child bond is inevitably secondary. This is not to say it is unimportant, but it is just not primary.

These born-again fathers also identified with the 'Couvade' – the custom amongst certain peoples whereby a man imitates the behaviour of his pregnant wife and at the time of birth is put to bed, as though he were having the baby. They spoke of 'an emotional solidarity' with their female partners by feeling sick during the pregnancy. This was the only time I agreed with them, although I only felt physically ill when I realized how much my children were going to cost me financially.

The most important finding of modern studies on fatherhood is that fathers can take a very central role in the emotional life and care of their children. Sebastian Kraemer, consultant child and family psychiatrist, in a chapter of the book *Gender, Power and Relationships*, states,

> We know that the most important qualities in a good father are not significantly different from those of a good mother. This does not mean that men and women have to be the same. On the contrary, the benefit of two involved parents is precisely because they are two different people and of different sexes . . . much of the research on the father's role points to the value of the child's relationship with the father, not because he is such a hero, or a big strong protector, a money-maker, or a terrifying disciplinarian but simply because he can be, and often is, supportive and warm with his children.

I thus wondered when researching this book and seeing that not many books or articles had been written by fathers exactly how the experience of having a child with Down's syndrome had affected them. I met and communicated with a number of them, who had children mainly under ten years old.

Contrary to popular belief, some men do actually want to talk about their feelings – maybe not quite so exhaustively and extensively as women, but we do still need to express our fears and concerns. This was certainly borne out by the number of fathers who were so willing to share their experiences so openly with me.

Despite the changing nature of the parental roles, there remains a stereotypical expectation of the father. We are still meant to be brave and strong and not be afraid. We must 'cope' whilst maintaining a sense of calm and logic and must also provide the principal source of emotional and practical sustenance. And yet we are also now expected to share our feelings and be honest in our fears and concerns. We are now allowed to show our pain. This dichotomy was keenly felt by a number of fathers, who stated that their main perceived role was to support their partners, wives and families and to be the ones who 'keep it all together'. Most of the fathers felt that they had to be 'responsible' and 'positive' in the face of adversity no matter how desperate they were feeling themselves.

One of the first tasks of the dad after the birth is to contact relatives and friends. When you have had a child with Down's syndrome, the task isn't quite so straightforward and the fathers I spoke to all found the experience extremely upsetting and very emotional.

One father said he 'told people in an apologetic way as if I was guilty of some kind of offence'. A number of the dads tried to be upbeat themselves to make it easier for the recipient of the phone call and one stated that he was deliberately cheerful in order to reassure everyone else. He wanted them to celebrate the child's birth as usual and tried to put them at their ease by being positive. Dominic Lawson said writing the article on his daughter, Domenica, was a very therapeutic exercise. Of all the fathers, his immediate reaction to his baby's birth was the most positive. One of 'intense, almost physically painful love'.

Whilst the audience to Dominic Lawson's news was rather large and his article was syndicated worldwide, the rest of the dads just notified friends and family by telephone. The general reaction was very positive, supportive and accepting. If any of these close contacts did have any negative feelings, they kept them to themselves at this stage, although some sent magazine and newspaper articles which were either binned straight away or hidden from wives! As one father wrote to me,

> Who would send an article about pregnancy in school girls to a
> new parent who had just given birth to a girl? If friends have
> just given birth to a blonde baby would it strike you as obvious
> to pass on a magazine article entitled, 'Blondes are at greater risk
> of dying of skin cancer'? Yet friends and family are obsessed with
> passing on any article that mentions 'Down's syndrome' in the
> title whether it bears any relevance to your stage of life or not!

Only one father knew that his child would be born with Down's syndrome and very few of the fathers (or indeed mothers) knew anything about Down's syndrome. Most of the parents knew the diagnosis within a few hours of the birth and the majority were told with sensitivity. Damon Hill, the former Formula One world champion, whose son, Oliver, has Down's syndrome, said, 'Hospital staff prepared us for the worst. We were told he might be able to perform menial tasks. Down's syndrome was portrayed as a family tragedy – he's enriched our lives beyond our wildest expectations.'

In another situation, the family was told by a junior doctor that he had 'some concerns' about the baby having Down's syndrome, but that this could not be confirmed until the consultant paediatrician could visit the next day. Having spent the whole night adjusting to this news, the following morning the parents were seen by another junior doctor, who looked at the baby and said that he did not think that the child did have Down's syndrome. The diagnosis was confirmed later that day by the consultant, but only after the parents had suffered a great deal of pain and confusion.

Reactions to the birth were a mixture of anxiety, devastation, confusion, sadness, disappointment and 'a sense of failure'. One father spoke of the surprise, then the shock, and then the disbelief. He immediately thought about how his wife would cope and what would his daughter do when she grew up? He then fainted! Another dad relates his feelings as an 'assault on our sensibilities' and this was a similar reaction by a father in *Uncommon Fathers*, an American book written by fathers about raising children with disabilities. One father describes the moment of realization that his son had Down's syndrome:

> Words were inadequate to describe this emotional cross-current: the peak of joy at the birth of my fine new son and the devastation at the death of my expectations. Moving back and forth between the extremes of emotional continuum *within the same second* is an experience reserved for few – fortunately. This powerful emotional oscillation between positive and negative emotions persists to this day – now slowly fading like the ear-splitting reverberation of a giant bell heard dangerously close.

Two fathers' immediate reactions were, 'No matter what he's like he's gorgeous and he's ours,' and 'We would love him just the same whatever happens.' The most positive responses came from fathers whose wives had had previous miscarriages or stillbirths and were relieved that their babies had been born safe and sound. The diagnosis of Down's syndrome was very much a secondary and less important factor in these dads' responses.

One father was traumatized and wanted his daughter 'to be taken away'. His mind was, however, swiftly changed by the attitude of his wife who accepted her newborn baby quickly and unreservedly. 'This immediate bond my wife had with this newborn child has become the most powerful and close relationship that I have witnessed in my entire life.'

I've heard of one dad who tried to smother his child and one who wished he could wave a magic wand and make the Down's syndrome disappear, but my favourite immediate response is exquisite in its simplicity and directness and has a universal male appeal. This father decided to take up karate because he wanted to make sure that no one was going to insult his son and get away with it!

Nearly all the fathers were certain that they would bring their babies home and in fact seemed to be more positive than some of the mothers. The general consensus was, 'In any event, who could look after him as well as we can?' and that the baby was 'better off with us than anyone else'.

After the initial shock, the fathers coped in myriad ways: they found solace in friends and family, the church, various support groups and a number read books on the subject to gain information. Whilst their wives and partners were trying to cope with it emotionally, some of the dads were attempting to absorb it intellectually. Generally it seems that the father felt pressure to get on with things as quickly as possible and immerse himself in the practicalities. 'I did all the washing and ironing – it helped me to find that there was some small domestic routine I could stay in control of when everything else seemed chaotic.' Another father described the first few months as a 'state of siege', having to 'batten down the hatches'.

Work played a large part in this adjustment as a way of

returning to some sort of normality. Of course some of the fathers had to return to their jobs very quickly after the birth and one or two felt that their most valuable contribution was that of provider, but it was also clear that they were relieved to use work as a way of escaping the stress at home.

In a survey on parents, Elaine Herbert reported responses to the disclosure of Down's syndrome by seven fathers whose children were born between 1986 and 1987. Health professionals who visited were much more concerned about how the mother was coping and very little attention was paid to the fathers. 'How's she taking it?' 'She may attempt suicide or harm the baby.' These fathers felt that they were thus marginalized, not even considered to need support themselves and just had to get on with it. I also found that the main role of the fathers I interviewed was that of propping up their partners, who, on the whole, took longer to accept what had happened.

Many of the fathers took on a very protective role and said that they felt much more sympathy for their wives. 'I felt sorry for my wife, who so wanted a daughter. Somehow I believed this thing we had brought into the world could never be a daughter. How wrong she has proved me.'

Due to the fact that it is the mothers who carry the child through pregnancy, it is they who take on the responsibility for what has happened. Many of the wives felt intensely unhappy, considering themselves 'failures', and felt guilty about having a child with Down's syndrome. The fathers were unable to remove the burden of responsibility from the mother and one father attempted a genetic approach:

> No amount of talking could get her out of her depression. She felt that it was her fault. There is no guilty party, but immediate acceptance of guilt by a woman is so well established in our culture that logic does not always work . . . the sex of the child is determined by the sperm not the egg. Simply because the

mother carries the baby and gives birth to it, why should she feel that she has 'failed' her husband if the sex is not the one he desired?

There is now also some evidence that the age of the father has some bearing on the foetus as it has been established that men have an increased risk of fathering a baby with Down's syndrome as they get older. Although we didn't discuss this specifically, no mention was made by the dads of any possible effect on their feelings of masculinity by fathering a child with disabilities.

When the child was born, there was general agreement that they had got the sex of the child that they had wanted. 'Glad he's a boy because he's less vulnerable to exploitation and won't get pregnant.' 'We wanted a girl so we were pleased.' 'We would have more anxieties about a girl. It's easier for a boy to fit in socially and be "one of the lads"' or 'I'm pleased that she's a girl – there is a belief that girls are more able.'

Of course there's likely to be a degree of rationalization in order to accept what has happened. We certainly did this with Sarah and spoke of how grateful we were that Sarah was the second born so that we had some experience of raising a child in ordinary circumstances before she arrived.

Whilst fathers are now taking more responsibility in child rearing and a significant share of nurturing, household duties are still considered less important than earning a living. Although things are changing, it is still true to say that it is predominantly the mother who takes the major role in the day to day care of the children. Despite two of the fathers who were house-husbands, the majority of fathers had work commitments which prevented them from playing a greater part in domestic events. The dads did, however, claim to be involved in special activities such as speech therapy, Makaton and Portage when possible.

Most of the fathers felt that they had experienced some fundamental changes to their outlook on life; the world was definitely felt to be a less benign place and most of the fathers felt increased feelings of insecurity. One dad described how it had made him more spiritual. He was now more affected by world events and the experience had put everything into perspective. He felt that his daughter's existence had given him a greater integrity. A father, the main aspect of whose job is communication, said that his daughter had helped him to communicate better. She had challenged his preconceptions of aesthetics and he said that he was now much more tolerant about levels of ability and achievement. He spoke of his intense relationship with his daughter, which had resulted in 'unconditional love'. He would never be the same person and stated, 'Only good has come out of the whole experience.'

Another father for whom work had been his main preoccupation decided to halve his salary and spend more time with his family. Not only did he feel less materialistic, but the ways in which he judged people changed. His previous heroes had been celebrated sportsmen, who had achieved greatness by their athletic prowess, but now he took greater pleasure in the small successes of unknown people. Those fathers who had judged their colleagues and friends by intellectual achievement now spoke of placing higher regard on other characteristics and nearly all said that they were generally much more tolerant and sympathetic.

Without question the overwhelming concern for the future was what would happen to their children with Down's syndrome when the parents were no longer around. One father said that he was so worried about his daughter being 'alone, rejected, isolated and discriminated against' that he felt he had to live until ninety so he could look after her! There was some concern about attendance at secondary schools where 'attitudes are harsher' and the possibility of abuse in future accommodation. Another father said, 'the only possible regret was to let go of dreams of early retirement and time with my wife without my five children'.

When I asked about why the fathers thought that this had happened to them, most replied it was just 'the luck of the draw', 'the cruelty and capriciousness of fate', 'just the way it is'. In one case it was a matter of 'God's way of trying to get your attention by giving you a slap around the head' and there was also talk of some 'fault' being involved, a feeling that it was divine retribution for past discrepancies. One man spent months and years desperately trying to find a reason why it had happened and wondered if he was being punished for doing something wrong. He had lived a fairly charmed life and was now 'paying the price'. No matter how much you love your child, there are times when all the extra worry and responsibility does seem like a heavy burden. In a quote from *Uncommon Fathers*, one father stated:

> When you don't believe in accidents or the random nature of life, you are left to accept full responsibility for everything that happens – good or bad. The pain caused by our son's medical problems was immense. Had we done this to him? Our feelings of guilt were tremendous . . . after I questioned why a 'good' God would do this to an innocent child, one friend angrily answered, 'Nobody said God is benevolent.'

This reminded me of one acquaintance who came to see us soon after Sarah's birth suggesting that it had something to do with Sarah's karma. His glib explanation was that everyone reaps what they sow for miscreant behaviour in previous existences. Sarah had probably done something in an earlier life and was now being punished. This was probably the most crass and insulting comment – among many – that we had heard and I was incensed.

None of the fathers, I'm glad to say, thought that they had been chosen for a special purpose and that only they could cope with this burden, although a couple did feel that it was some sort of a test – not necessarily of a spiritual nature, but more of a life experience. Without question it was the families whose children also suffered from medical problems who experienced the most disruption to their lives and one dad, whose child was quite ill for the first year of her life, said his wife was 'astonished' at how well he coped with two other children!

Every father stated that despite the extra stress, pressure and general fatigue, he felt closer to his partner and this actually concurs with a number of studies which show that the level of marital disharmony and the rate of separation and divorce is no higher among parents who have a child with Down's syndrome.

Whilst researching this chapter there were a few incidents and comments told to me, which although unrelated, deserve recounting for their humour, sadness and honesty.

An eight-year-old girl with Down's syndrome visited her grandfather in a hospice just a few weeks before he died and told the nursing staff to be 'very very gentle with my granddad'.

One daughter insisted that her father kissed the family's extremely ugly and slobbery boxer dog each day before going to work!

'The best moment was when my sister, who lives in America, said she had joined the local Down's syndrome support group.'

'The real low point for me was leaving my son in Intensive Care while having to go to my father's funeral – he had died from head injuries sustained falling from a bus on his way home from visiting my mum who was in hospital with a broken leg.'

'I hadn't been able to accept my daughter at all and didn't think I could ever love her. This changed completely when my two other children saw her for the first time and fell in love with her straightaway.'

When visiting a baby of a few months, a health visitor handed out a supply of fluoride tablets to the surprised parents who were told by way of explanation, 'Retarded children always have rotten teeth.'

A six-year-old girl whose mother was expecting a baby had been reading a book for some time, entitled My Special Needs Sister. When her mother finally did give birth to a daughter and the girl was going to the hospital to meet her new sister, she told her father that the baby would need this book. She had not been told that her sister had Down's syndrome and the family had not known of the diagnosis prior to the birth...

'It was wonderful when we took her to hospital to meet her new brother. Her eyes lit up as we sat on the bed and she immediately demanded that we place the baby on her knee for a cuddle. She then proceeded to check all his features and gave us a big grin as she named each part in turn. She also seemed to understand that he was her brother and fully accepted him as part of the family.'

The eight-year-old cousin of a baby born with Down's syndrome said, 'At least something interesting has happened in the family.' (This coincidentally is exactly what Sarah's grandmother – also aged eight at the time – said when her father was carted off to a German concentration camp.)

A friend's elderly mother said what a beautiful baby he was and then asked the parents how much longer they were going to keep him...

The horrified reaction of a father when he discovered that the landlord of a local pub refused to serve a customer with learning difficulties when he visited with a carer. (I was equally shocked when I heard of a hotelier who had refused to accommodate a family with a child with Down's syndrome.)

A father heard a midwife say, 'I would let children like that die.'

'When my daughter was seven months old, we went to Paris and saw Professor Lejeune [discoverer of the chromosomal imbalance]. It was his manner with her and us – I almost said his aura, for he radiated calm and hope – that was so powerful, so moving. It was a privilege sadly no longer available to others.'

'The worst moment for me was when I arrived at the hospital to see my daughter who had a serious heart condition and I saw the nurses crying. I knew that my daughter had died.'

'In many ways the distressing thing about having a child with Down's syndrome is not the reality, but the fact that what keeps most parents buoyed up is the idea that their own baby Johnny is going to be an Einstein. No-one is ever going to give birth to most of the normal people we see around us every day, but by the time little Johnny is struggling to pass his A-levels, one is well beyond these dreams and more at ease with the reality of normal life. The parents of a baby with Down's syndrome are denied all these dreams and instead have a different reality held up in front of them. They are as able to cope with this picture as is the father in the next maternity ward if he were told that his new daughter was going to spend much of her adult life as a cashier behind the till. But in twenty years' time he may be very happy to know that his daughter had a secure job and was enjoying her life.'

Following Sarah's birth, Allie felt a strong need to meet with other parents in similar situations and gained a huge amount of support through this contact. At the time she tried in vain to encourage me to join her in a parents' group or to meet some of the mothers and their partners. I firmly resisted these offers believing, and I'm sure rightly at the time, that there could be no value in such an exercise for me.

I was taken aback, therefore, when researching this book, to discover the power that communicating with other fathers held – whether in person, on the telephone or through correspondence. As I heard of their feelings of confusion, fear and helplessness as well as their love and tenderness for their children, I relived many of my own emotions and felt an extraordinary closeness to these men. Most of them were complete strangers whom I might never even meet face to face and probably with nothing else in common apart from our children's extra chromosome.

Nevertheless, their insights and honesty were absolutely fascinating and their willingness and ability to share these emotions with me have been yet another unforgettable experience.

20. Let's Face it, She Won't be a Big Earner

My apprehensions come in crowds:
I dread the rustling of the grass:
The very shadows of the clouds
Have power to shake me as they pass:
I question things and do not find
One that will answer to my mind:
And all the world appears unkind.
(William Wordsworth,
'The Affliction of Margaret')

In January 1996, Sarah was a bridesmaid at the wedding of her BBC producer Gareth Edwards and Frances Wedgwood. We were greatly touched that Sarah should be so honoured, but due to the conventions of the occasion, slightly wary of other people's reactions to her and what they might think. Would they realize that Sarah has Down's syndrome and what, if anything, would it mean to them? Did we want to announce to all that Sarah had Down's syndrome so that any errant behaviour might be excused or should we just keep quiet and let her be herself? We needn't have worried. Everyone at this rather grand affair was extremely kind and thoughtful and the two adult bridesmaids looked after Sarah admirably. Despite the focus of attention and the freezing temperatures, Sarah carried out her duties beautifully.

It is, however, occasions such as these that make us all think of the important landmarks in our lives. We reflect upon our own rights of passage and then the expectations that we have of our children. In Sarah's case, it raises a lot of anxiety and fear and one of the most difficult things about parenting a child with Down's syndrome is the prospect of a very uncertain future.

Of course, parents worry about their children all their lives, but one can afford a certain optimism at the prospect of your children being able to lead fulfilling and contented lives. I'm quietly confident when I think of Daniel's and Joel's future, but as soon as Sarah was diagnosed as having Down's syndrome, we were immediately forced to consider serious issues for the future.

Although we did adapt to the philosophy of coping with Sarah stage by stage, we couldn't help thinking of how things were going to be in one, two, five, or even twenty or fifty years' time. Would she be independent? Would she work? Have relationships? Have sex? Would Sarah marry? Become a mother? Drive? Vote? Develop particular illnesses? Die early? We were already thinking about her life expectancy when we should have just been concentrating on changing her nappies.

There are also the more immediate concerns and day to day uncertainties relating to when we allow or encourage certain stages of independence. When should we let Sarah cross the road without supervision . . . allow her to go to school unaccompanied . . . or let her stay 'home alone'? It is extremely hard to be clear about these decisions with any child, but it is much more difficult when her chronological age may not concur with Sarah's capabilities.

As we sat in the beautiful Surrey village church and watched Frances, adorned and adored, Allie and I were both wondering whether Sarah would ever experience the joy and happiness that Frances clearly felt that day. Of course I wouldn't mind not having to foot the bill for such a fabulous wedding, but I do hope to see Sarah with a partner one day – if that's what she wants – and I am heartened to hear of relationships and marriages of people who have Down's syndrome. There are times, however, when adults with learning disabilities do find true romance and maintain a relationship only to be at the mercy of prejudice and ignorance.

In 1995 there was an attempt by the father of a woman with Down's syndrome to have her marriage annulled in the High Court. The woman had married another man with Down's syndrome, whom she had known for four years before they decided to legalize their relationship.

Anna Russell's father, who allegedly had not seen her for several years, tried to have the marriage annulled on the grounds that her disability prevented her from making rational decisions. Fortunately for Anna and her husband Matthew, the application was withdrawn when incontrovertible evidence proved that Anna was totally capable of making decisions about her own life. Anna Russell's solicitor, Lydia Sinclair, stated, 'We were ready to contest the action on the grounds that it was a serious intrusion into the private lives of this young couple and no business of the courts. We are happy this will no longer be necessary.'

It was through Anna seeking legal advice and taking the initiative to instruct a solicitor that the marriage remained legal. One wonders how many other couples in similar situations would not have had the opportunity to pursue their rights through the courts.

We also wonder what is going to happen to Sarah when she starts to take an interest in boys? (I'm taking a heterosexual approach here – purely for convenience sake – if she is gay, then so be it, although I have to say the pressure of being the Martina Navratilova of the Down's world might just be too much for one person.) Will Sarah's affections be reciprocated? Will boys take an interest in her or will she be constantly rejected? Will she be more vulnerable to unsuitable advances?

There's a lovely conversation in *Count Us In* in which Mitchell Levitz and Jason Kingsley (both of whom have Down's syndrome) discuss asking a girl out. Mitchell responds to the question as to whether he had ever asked a girl without learning difficulties out to dinner or a movie:

Mitchell: Yes, I did once. I was rejected. Not because of the disability or anything. Because she was seeing somebody else ... It's okay to be friends and socialize, but it's not okay to go up to a woman and expect everything that you want ... The important thing is, Jason, that if you want to know her, all you have to do is be nice to her and talk to her and get to know her. Then you'll have a better way, a better sense of what's in common to do things together...

Jason: I might do that for the future. I could go up to a girl and say, 'Hi. How are you, what's your name? Maybe when we get older we could have a date together. A weekend.'

Mitchell: I don't think a woman wants to be asked if you want to spend a weekend. You'd be better off asking her to a movie, not a weekend. It would be better to get to know her first.

Jason: I might have to say, 'What's school like? What are your studies? What do you think about me? What do you think can be changed in our lives? How are you getting along with your boyfriend?' Or something.

Mitchell: Be serious.

Jason: Okay, I'll be serious. 'Where have you been all your life?'

Up until fairly recently, the whole subject of disabled people having sex was taboo and as extraordinary as it may seem in the 1990s, sex education still remains a contentious issue. Parents still have a right to withdraw their children from sex education classes and as Sarah Boston says, 'Giving sex education to people with learning difficulties touches not just on a question of sexual morality, it touches on the question of the rights of people with learning difficulties to be human beings in every sense of the word.'

One area that I have yet to worry about, but one that I know Allie already thinks about a great deal, is whether Sarah will become a mother or not. It is so painful for Allie that she has not been able to face researching this subject in any depth. For Allie, motherhood was always one of her main aims in life and she would want Sarah also to have this most wonderful experience. On the other hand, how would Sarah cope with such responsibility? Would the baby have Down's syndrome? (Apparently there is a one in three chance that it would.) Would this matter? Would we have wishes or rights to intervene?

Sarah loves playing with her dolls and at one stage even used to pretend to breastfeed them when Allie was doing the same with Joel. It is hard to think that Sarah may be deprived of motherhood – purely because she has an extra chromosome. In this particular situation, does extra means less?

I suppose the general and rather obvious conclusion is that we want Sarah to live as 'normal' a life as possible. As parents, we no doubt use our own lives as guidelines for our children's lives. The identification that we have with them is inescapable. This may mean we would like our offspring to emulate our own lives or indeed lead very opposite existences. Within this wish we have to be realistic about details; the type of job that may fulfil Sarah may not have fulfilled me. Her choice of partner may not be the 'ideal' man. This could of course apply to parents of any child as all children are true individuals and quite rightly we do not have the power to mould exact replicas, but perhaps we will need to be more flexible and accepting of Sarah's choices in these matters.

We have always been clear that we would wish Sarah to be independent of us in the same way as Daniel and Joel and in order to be able to achieve this, the attainment of accommodation and employment is absolutely vital. As tempting as it would be to keep Sarah safe by continuing to have her live with us when she is an adult, this would inevitably prevent her from leading her own, individual life. There is a fine balance between protection and stifling. And even more worrying, what would happen to her when we were no longer around?

Once she is an adult, we will encourage her to move to whatever type of housing is most suitable. We hope that Sarah might be able to manage a flat of her own or a place that she could share with friends. There are also various organizations which provide accommodation for whole communities. Although I would obviously prefer to see Sarah completely integrated, this sort of provision does at least provide security and stability in a semi-independent setting where she would have the opportunity to make a positive contribution to a community.

The idea of a group home where a number of people with learning disabilities can live together is also an option, although I do worry about the attitude of some people who live near these homes. We have all seen what happens when plans are unveiled to open a hostel or group home and local residents, acting out of ignorance and prejudice, endeavour to prevent this happening. In a recent news story, local people clubbed together to buy a house which was earmarked as a group home, to prevent adults with learning difficulties from moving in.

I suppose the most worrying scenario would be if Sarah wasn't capable of living even in a semi-independent setting and had to live in an institution. If we are trying to integrate those with Down's syndrome into mainstream schooling, employment and all possible facets of 'normal' life, then we should no longer consider housing them all together for convenience sake. There is also the worry about abuse in some of these establishments and although I am positive these incidents are rare and that most of the care is safe and good, it is something that parents of children with disabilities worry most about. It was pointed out to us by an acquaintance soon after Sarah was born. 'Of course, it won't get any easier as Sarah grows up as "handicapped" adults are always being abused' we were cheerfully reminded, before he went on to describe a litany of cases that he had heard about.

In a recent issue of the Down's syndrome newsletter, parents wrote about their daughter of twenty-six living in a group home, who had been abused by a member of staff. Despite an initial confession of guilt, the man wasn't convicted because the woman's parents felt that she would not be able to undergo a traumatizing court appearance in which she would have to give evidence and be cross-examined. She was likely to be torn apart by defence solicitors and there was no possibility of giving evidence by video link.

The key to decent accommodation is of course the ability to be able to pay for it – not just from state benefits, but from proper wages. The title of this chapter was prompted by a friend of Allie's, who was discussing the job prospects of her own daughter with Down's syndrome and stated in an unintentionally humorous way the reality of the situation.

Although many people with Down's syndrome are capable of holding down a variety of jobs, when there are periods of recession and high unemployment it is somewhat unlikely that they will be able to compete fairly with the 'able-bodied' in the job market. People with disabilities are likely to suffer discrimination and despite the fact that there is legislation that requires 3 per cent of the people employed by a firm or an organization to be disabled, this just doesn't happen.

Of course being employed doesn't just mean being able to have money for decent housing and standard of living. It also provides you with choices about your lifestyle and pursuance of leisure activities and means that you can feel valued whilst contributing to society. The workplace is where you make friends, where you can realize some of your aspirations and where, most importantly, people with learning disabilities can feel independent.

The financial implications of having a child with Down's syndrome are considerable and it is another area where one is forced to think of the long-term future. Sadly, Sarah is not likely to be financially independent and will need help from us, and her brothers and other family members during her life.

An interesting issue, currently under debate, is that of voting rights of the learning disabled. Contrary to popular belief, people with learning difficulties are entitled to vote, but only about 5 per cent of them do so.

In 1996, Mencap launched a national awareness campaign to encourage people with learning disabilities to register to vote. It was made quite clear that this was not an attempt to force people to vote, but to ensure that those who were capable of registering were given the opportunity. Mencap identified Britain's thirty-seven most marginal seats, which could have been won or lost by the swing votes of people with learning disabilities. Of course, due to the Labour Party's landslide victory in May 1997, these figures were untested, but it was, all the same, a fascinating proposition.

Mencap produced a leaflet with an explanation of the parliamentary process, a glossary of terms and instructions about what to do in the polling booth. When Sarah reaches the age of eighteen, I would hope that she has the same opportunity to exert her democratic right as everybody else and, in this way, make a contribution to the political system that makes laws about what she can and cannot do. I feel sure that if Sarah continues to absorb as much knowledge as she has been and the issues are explained to her in a straightforward and clear manner, she would be quite able to decide whom to vote for.

The reaction to this campaign was, in some quarters, surprisingly virulent. An article in the *Sunday Telegraph* in June 1997, written by Minette Marrin entitled 'A step too far for the handicapped', stated in extraordinarily patronizing terms that the 'handicapped were being forced to lead normal lives by "professional carers" and "well intentioned progressives"'.

In a blanket statement she concluded, 'the mentally handicapped should not be allowed to vote'. Nor, according to the article, should they be allowed to marry, have children or 'take on rights and duties' they cannot possibly fulfil. Of course all 'people with learning disabilities' – a term she dismisses as 'misleading' – are generalized as having the same abilities and intelligence.

One wonders which other sections of society she might also like to disenfranchise. Perhaps residents of old people's homes, who are all institutionalized and therefore incapable of looking after themselves, should be stripped of their democratic rights. Maybe people who are blind shouldn't be allowed to vote, as they obviously can't see where to put the cross on the ballot paper. Or should we continue to treat them as individuals and assist them in participating in the society in which they live?

It is unfortunate that Ms Marrin seems unable to understand the fact that some people with learning disabilities are in a position to decide for themselves about their rights and are not coerced by well-meaning but ultimately naive do-gooders to carry this through. They need assistance to pursue these goals, but I expect even Ms Marrin needs help with certain tasks. She goes on to say that 'wishful thinking' will not change 'the tragedy of mental handicap'. Perhaps not, but this sort of prejudice is just the kind of opinion that will forever cause discrimination and pain to people with disability.

We know it won't be long now before Sarah herself begins to understand that she is different and have some grasp about what it means to have Down's syndrome. If she does have any idea at the moment, using her level of confidence as a yardstick, I can only suggest that she sees it as a positive thing. She was recently listening to an episode of *Minor Adjustment* and heard the words 'a Down's syndrome child'. She pointed to herself proudly and said, 'Me!'

In due course, however, she may have other feelings about it. The subject is obviously discussed very openly in our home, but we will not force her to talk about it. She is still too young to understand all the implications, but is obviously already aware that she has extra help at school, has speech therapy and attends more hospital appointments than most children. She has to have regular eye tests and although she is not the only child in her class to wear glasses, the fact that she is long-sighted is probably the result of having Down's syndrome.

It is important that Sarah is aware of what it means to have Down's syndrome and knows it is not her fault that she cannot keep up with her peers. She must be given the opportunity to discuss her disability, which should help to minimize some of the confusing feelings that she is bound to experience. She will always have Down's syndrome and not talking about it won't make it go away.

As Sarah grows up, she may not be able to compare with the achievements or cope with the conversations and intellectual abilities of her friends who may well be much more sophisticated than her. She may not be able to communicate as well as them and may become frustrated at her inability to achieve the things that she really wants to achieve.

Sarah will not be oblivious to her limitations and one might think that this could actually make things more difficult for her. Adults whose level of ability precludes them from being cognisant of their condition may not suffer the anguish of being aware that they are somehow limited. In fact research shows that children and adults who know they have Down's syndrome actually have higher self-esteem than those who are unaware of their diagnosis. They have actually come to terms with the fact that they are different and in some cases are proud of it.

Although, at the present time, we are not completely aware of the limits to what Sarah can achieve, we know that there *are* limits. And yet, a major part of the adjustment we began to make at Sarah's birth was that our expectations were diminished. Looking at it in this way, all of Sarah's achievements are a bonus.

Living with an uncertain future is part and parcel of being

alive and there is no question that we have specific fears and anxieties in relation to Sarah. We cannot make everything right for her. We can only give her opportunities and help her to be secure. Then she will have to cope with her own limitations.

Sarah herself, of course, has no such worries at the moment. Like most children she lives for the moment and when I am in her presence, I am always amazed by her own sense of self. She is direct and honest and her heart is not just worn on her sleeve, she seems to be attired fully in a suit of many emotional colours for all to see. Her confidence is rock solid. She certainly does not need us to worry for her. If this is at the core of her spirit, then all will surely be well.

Even in the 1970s, the scenario for parents of children with Down's syndrome was extremely bleak. From the moment of birth, it was assumed that you wouldn't take your newborn baby home and if you did, parents were told that their children would never be able to walk, talk, dress themselves, have meaningful thoughts or accomplish anything.

It is only during the last twenty years – through the strength and conviction of parents who were brave and strong enough to disagree with negative medical advice – that any positive changes have come about. Although we still have a long way to go in changing society's view of the disabled and in the pursuance of total acceptance, there is beginning to exist a greater awareness of Down's syndrome. Sarah's generation is the first that has not been written off completely at birth. There is now an expectation of a life fulfilled.

21. A Suitable Case for Treatment?

> Gladly we desire to make other men perfect, but we will not
> amend our own fault.
>
> (Thomas Kempis, 1426)

The United States Air Force Delta Two space rocket, which was to launch a satellite in January 1997, blew into smithereens in a huge explosion, which filled the skies with flames and black acrid smoke. As the wreckage from the multi-million dollar rocket started to plummet to earth, a voice from mission control in Cape Canaveral was heard to say, 'We have an anomaly.'

A chromosomal anomaly is how Down's syndrome is sometimes described – a simple explanation for a very complex condition.

The Down's Syndrome Association states:

> Any couple can have a baby with Down's syndrome and it
> occurs in families from all social, economic, cultural, religious
> and racial backgrounds. As Down's syndrome is present from
> the time of conception, nothing a woman does in pregnancy will
> influence whether or not her baby has Down's syndrome.
> Nothing is known which could have stopped the parent giving
> an extra chromosome. The chance of having a baby with
> Down's syndrome increases with parental age. However, more
> babies are born to younger women as the overall birth-rate is
> higher in this age group.
>
> There is no evidence that diet, medicines, illnesses or
> upbringing have any influence on whether or not a parent can or
> will have a child with Down's syndrome.

Each year about 700 babies are born with Down's syndrome – about one in every 1,000 births. It is the most common cause of learning disability and there are an estimated 30,000 people with Down's syndrome living in the United Kingdom.

No one has discovered what causes the chromosomal anomaly that leads to Down's syndrome, but it is known that individuals with Down's syndrome have an extra chromosome. For some unexplained reason, an error in cell development results in forty-seven chromosomes instead of the normal forty-six.

Down's syndrome is also known as **Trisomy 21** because the extra genetic material is usually located in the twenty-first pair of chromosomes. In about 4 per cent of cases, Down's syndrome is caused by the presence of an extra part rather than a whole chromosome (**Translocation**), and the most rare form of Down's syndrome is **Mosaicism** where there is an extra chromosome twenty-one in only a proportion of the body cells and where the rest of the cells are normal.

The genetic imbalance that results from the additional chromosome affects both mental and physical development. There are about one hundred characteristic features of Down's syndrome, which may or may not present themselves in any one individual. Some of the characteristics are slightly slanting almond-shaped eyes, which often have a fold of skin running vertically between the two lids (the epicanthic fold), a head which is rather flat at the back of the hairline and ill-defined at the nape of the neck, hands which are broader than average with short fingers and an unusual crease on one or both of the palms. There is sometimes a deep cleft between the first and second toes.

About 40 per cent of children with Down's syndrome have a high rate of congenital heart defects which sometimes need surgery, and the most common physical problems are hypotonia (a general floppiness in muscle tone) and respiratory infections (colds, coughs, ear and throat infections). Hearing loss occurs more frequently and children with Down's syndrome are at greater risk of having visual impairments in early childhood.

It is estimated that between 5 and 10 per cent of people with Down's syndrome suffer some form of epilepsy – higher than in the general population – and there is evidence of a greater risk of developing symptoms of Alzheimer's-like dementia at an early age.

It is likely that up to 30 per cent of people with Down's syndrome may develop thyroid disease and they are also more likely to develop Celiac disease – an absorption problem in the small bowel due to an overexposure to gluten.

Children with Down's syndrome have a much greater risk (about twenty times) of developing leukaemia. Not only is the risk greater, but the peak age of leukaemia deaths in children is four years, but in children with Down's syndrome it is one year.

Developmental delays are evident from the early months of life in terms of children being able to turn over, sit, stand and walk. The delay in speech and language is even more marked – the reasons for which are still not fully understood.

Up until about fifty years ago, the majority of people with Down's syndrome were not expected to reach adulthood and those who did survive lived in institutions, where treatment of physical ailments connected to their diagnosis was negligible or at best rudimentary. With greater medical involvement, educational opportunity and a greater awareness of the condition, the average life expectancy of people with Down's syndrome has changed radically. In the 1940s, it was nine years old. In the early 1960s it was eighteen and it is now somewhere between sixty and seventy. Despite the fact that there has been great progress, it is still heartbreaking when you realize that your child's life may be reduced so dramatically and she may have about twenty years less to live than the 'average' person.

Sarah did not have much hair when she was born, but amongst her few blonde locks we discovered, to our surprise, a single strand of silver hair. This streak of grey has remained and is now a constant reminder that her ageing process is speeded up by her having Down's syndrome.

One of the things that we had read about when Sarah was very young was that people with Down's syndrome are likely to develop some form of dementia at an earlier than normal age and the fact that a hair had already turned grey at birth was a terrifying warning of things to come.

The likelihood of people with Down's syndrome being affected by Alzheimer's disease is one which causes much distress to parents and yet still remains somewhat unclear. It seems that there is a large number of people with Down's syndrome who do suffer from Alzheimer's-like symptoms, but these may not be of an organic nature.

According to consultant psychiatrist Tony Holland (adviser to the Down's Syndrome Association), 'In Down's syndrome, it has been recognised since the early 1900's that changes in the brain are observed from relatively early in life. The vast majority of people with Down's syndrome do have evidence of Alzheimer's-like disease in their brains when they are in their forties.' However, it seems that the symptoms of Alzheimer's do not appear so severe in Down's syndrome and Dr Holland goes on to say, 'the changes that are present may have no effect on the person's functioning'.

Dementia due to Alzheimer's disease is a steadily progressive disorder with evidence of decline over time and this deterioration in memory or behaviour is extremely difficult to diagnose in someone with Down's syndrome, who may exhibit some of these traits for other reasons which may well be environmental or social.

There is much research being done into Alzheimer's disease, which may benefit people with Down's syndrome, but to the best of my knowledge at the present time, there have been no specific trials of the treatment of Alzheimer's in people with Down's syndrome.

So far there is no known treatment which can prevent brain cells dying, but there is much discussion about whether the potential for Alzheimer's disease can be modified through dietary supplements or other means and whether the use of vitamins can prevent increased oxidization and damage to brain cells. This discussion has implications for an even more controversial issue that is currently raging within the Down's syndrome world.

There is a debate that has gone on for a number of years that some of the disabilities caused by Down's syndrome can develop in the months and years after birth due to metabolic imbalances, and can therefore be treated. Many children and adults with Down's syndrome have mineral and vitamin deficiencies and TNI (Targeted Nutritional Intervention) which is a therapy designed primarily but not exclusively for children with Down's syndrome, can supposedly correct these imbalances. The treatment comprises supplements of vitamins, minerals, amino acids and digestive enzymes and is based on a nutritional programme designed in the United States about forty years ago by Dr Henry Turkel.

Of course, you don't have to have Down's syndrome to suffer from nutritional deficiencies, which can cause problems with behaviour, learning, growth and general health. If there are vitamin deficiencies then of course they should be addressed, but then that applies to everyone in society. As with any child, I would say that good health, balanced nutrition and the optimum social and educational opportunities create the best environment for maximizing development.

There is, however, much anecdotal evidence from parents about how their children have made significant progress and in May 1996, more than 12,000 individuals with Down's syndrome in the United States were using TNI. According to these parents and supportive physicians, cognitive development and speech can be improved, general behaviour ameliorated and there is talk of physical characteristics being changed.

This therapeutic approach is sometimes supplemented by the use of Piracetam. Piracetam, which is unlicensed both in the United Kingdom and the United States for use with children, is a 'smart drug' which allegedly improves intellectual performance and enhances memory and learning. I have this picture of children with Down's syndrome, who have excelled beyond expectation in school examinations, being picked out for random drug tests and then when traces of substances are discovered in their blood, are banned from participation in further educational enterprises until they go 'straight'.

Although there may be anecdotal and testimonial claims of success, further research is required. There is no scientific evidence and there have been no strictly controlled studies to confirm that there is improved mental functioning, decreased hypotonia or improved speech following TNI treatment. This treatment is expensive and so it is likely that the parents who are using it are financially more comfortable, in a better environment, better educated and with more opportunities for greater resources. The 'social class' effect has an even greater significance for children with disabilities.

Piracetam also has recognized side effects such as hyperactivity, nervousness, depression and insomnia and the long-term effects of such high levels of supplementation of minerals and vitamins are not known.

One of the other claims of TNI is the improvement of facial features, although the word 'improvement' does make me somewhat nervous, as the term can only be subjective and dictated by society's desire to make everyone appear 'normal'. However, there is no doubt that age actually has the same effect. When I look back at pictures of Sarah as a baby, the Down's syndrome features were much more pronounced than they are now at the age of five.

We think Sarah is beautiful just the way she is and although the 'stigmata' have softened, her physiognomy remains unmistakably that of a child with Down's syndrome. The degree to which this is the case seems to depend upon her expression, her level of tiredness and the angle of view. Her Down's syndrome is a part of her very being so we do not wish to take that away from her and in any case, her unique character is so prominent that her features become irrelevant.

Another argument currently raging is about the rights and wrongs of facial plastic surgery to dilute the outward signs of Down's syndrome in children.

Operations of this kind were first performed in Argentina in the 1970s. They are now quite varied and include the following: skin folds around the eyes are pulled back; ears are pinned back; the nose is narrowed; the chin is built up and cheekbones are made more prominent. Some of these operations have been performed on children as young as three years old.

An operation involving a reduction in the size of the tongue became popular in the early 1980s. Children with Down's syndrome often have small mouths and larger than average tongues. This can mean that the tongue appears too large and can protrude. There are simple methods that can be employed to teach a child to keep his tongue inside his mouth. However, if the habit persists after a certain age, a tongue reduction operation might be considered. This involves quite a major surgical procedure, but there are claims that there have been additional improvements in speech clarity and breathing functions as a result.

There is, of course, a difference between surgery undertaken for a therapeutic effect and that performed for purely cosmetic reasons. No operation is without risk and no amount of cosmetic surgery will prevent the consequences, varied as they are, of having Down's syndrome. If, as parents – for it is the parents who make these decisions – we are trying to eradicate the physical characteristics as a way of denying the diagnosis, then are we also admitting that we cannot accept our children for who they are? Are we trying to hide our children's identity in the hope that we can make them appear more 'normal'?

Everybody has his or her own individual personality and physical make-up. Sarah has her own features and her own personality. We would only be changing the way she looks to make her features more acceptable to other people. Yet again, the onus should be on society to come to terms with the way that it treats children and adults with Down's syndrome and not the person who needs to change. A parallel argument may run for other oppressed minority groups in our society. Is the solution for black people to take advantage of some future technology to biochemically engineer themselves to whiteness? Who would ever want to surgically shed their race? Well, OK there is allegedly one notable exception . . . but we won't have a word said against him, in this house.

Perhaps a child who cannot know there is something 'amiss' with his or her appearance may begin to wonder – perhaps for the first time – what was wrong with the way he or she looks anyway. Hence a child could develop a self-consciousness which could be especially unhelpful to someone who in society's narrow terms may never be considered classically good-looking. Some people also suggest that it can be useful for a child or adult to possess the recognizable physical features of the syndrome so that there is a greater understanding of why the behaviour might be different.

It is, however, a complicated area and there are some views that I do think are valid. We are all guilty of wanting to make ourselves appear as attractive as we can and even if we know this is just due to socialization of the 'cultural norms', this doesn't stop us from trying to look younger by dyeing our hair, trying to lose weight or wearing the latest fashions. The way we look is important to us. Why shouldn't it be so for adults and children with Down's syndrome? If they don't want to have ears that stick out, why should the fact that they have Down's syndrome prevent them from surgery like everyone else?

It has been stated that cosmetic surgery in children with Down's syndrome has nothing to do with parental vanity. Rather, all parents want what is best for their children and if this means protecting them in whatever way from the ignorance and cruelty of the world around them, then this is one way of doing it. Although I do believe, as stated, that it is society that should change, one parent, whose seven-year-old daughter went through cosmetic surgery, was reported as saying, 'It's easier to change one person than to change the world.'

In *Past, Present and Future,* Brian Stratford chooses a George Bernard Shaw quote to summarize his own thoughts about this issue: 'The reasonable man adapts himself to the world: the unreasonable one persists in trying to adapt the world to himself. Therefore all progress depends on the unreasonable man.'

Overall, I'm with Messrs Shaw and Stratford on this one but I'm left wondering whether the great man would have considered adapting his maxim in any way, if he had to address some of the secondary dilemmas facing a parent in making the kinds of decisions discussed here.

If Sarah does decide to have plastic surgery when she is old enough to make her own mind up, we would support her in that decision. Whilst she is a child, however, we wouldn't ever try to change her appearance in the hope that her quality of life might be enriched. Trying to improve Sarah's cognitive ability is, of course, not quite so straightforward. Despite the fact that there is undoubtedly a greater awareness about Down's syndrome in general, there has actually been very little research into cognitive intervention.

The Down Syndrome Educational Trust (DownsEd) – in partnership with the University of Portsmouth – promotes the development and education of children with Down's syndrome. Based at the Sarah Duffen Centre in Portsmouth, the Trust has been engaged in research, services, training and publishing since 1980 and is now an internationally renowned centre. Named after a young woman with Down's syndrome, whose father's account of her early reading progress inspired the first research project, the centre offers an advisory service for parents and teachers. Research has been used to inform the development and evaluation of intervention programmes to help children overcome their learning difficulties.

Sue Buckley, who is Professor of Psychology of Developmental Disability at the Sarah Duffen Centre, sees language and speech as essential in the intervention and integration process and believes that any child with a language delay will therefore be at risk for delay in all areas of cognitive or mental development. 'The aim is to understand the reasons for delayed development in children with Down's syndrome in order to develop optimally effective remedial and educational strategies for them. It is simply not good enough to accept that children cannot do certain things because they have Down's syndrome, we want to know why that is and then do something about it.'

The trust is the focus of a dynamic programme of research where there are currently five doctorates in progress. Projects have focused on uncovering the underlying reasons for developmental delay and then evaluating remedial strategies. A recent study into sleep disturbance showed that the sleep problems of children with Down's syndrome are predominantly physical in origin and are related to disordered breathing. There was a clear link between sleep disorders and moodiness, irritability and poor cognitive function during the day.

This is just one example where research can raise awareness, change effective treatment and expel such myths as the only reason why adolescents with Down's syndrome sometimes exhibit poor behaviour is because . . . they have Down's syndrome.

Of course every form of treatment, be it convenient or controversial is governed by environments and monetary implications. None more so than in surgical transplants. Fortunately Sarah does not suffer from a congenital heart condition, but I wonder what would happen if she ever did require serious heart surgery.

Joanne Harris is a fourteen-year-old girl who needs a heart and lung transplant and was the subject of a Channel Four documentary, *A Heart For Jo*, in 1996. Joanne has a hole in her heart and her condition can only be cured by a transplant. In a world where able-bodied patients have to compete for limited resources, children and adults with disabilities are low on the priority list. Their lives are subject to value judgements that the Patients Charter doesn't admit to.

Although it is common practice for children with Down's syndrome to undergo heart surgery, no child with Down's syndrome has ever been assessed for a heart and lung transplant. Apparently, when it comes to disabled people, intellectual ability is a major factor in deciding whether or not a patient deserves a new heart. The 'able-bodied' aren't yet asked to undergo an IQ test before being accepted for medical treatment.

If Jo had undergone cardiac surgery soon after her birth it is likely that she would not now need a transplant, but babies with Down's syndrome born in previous decades were discriminated against. It has just been revealed that babies and young children with Down's syndrome who were living in institutions were used as guinea pigs by British doctors in 1960 to test an experimental vaccine for measles. And even today, there are some cardiac paediatricians who are reluctant to operate on children with Down's syndrome.

In the United States similar situations exist. Sandra Jensen was a thirty-five-year-old woman with Down's syndrome who was living independently, but due to a congenital heart defect needed a heart and lung transplant to stay alive. In 1995, Stanford University Hospital rejected her request for treatment on the grounds that people with Down's syndrome are not 'appropriate' candidates for heart and lung transplants. A hospital in San Diego turned her down as she was 'limited in her ability to have recall and memory'. One doctor asked Sandra why she wanted the operation and when Sandra replied, 'Because I want to live,' he reportedly said, 'That's not a good enough reason.'

Following a public outcry, the operation was completed in January 1996 and Ms Jensen was reported to be 'the first seriously retarded person in the United States to receive a major transplant'. Sadly Sandra died in May 1997 whilst undergoing surgery to remove a blood clot. Her death was not a result of complications of the transplant and in fact she lived for longer than many heart and lung transplant patients.

The British Medical Society is based on the ethic that the needs of the individual are paramount and whilst we are striving to obtain educational, employment and other rights for children and adults with Down's syndrome, these must also be extended to equal medical treatment.

Of course one is not oblivious to the desperately precious resources of donated organs. Until there is a co-ordinated programme, there will continue to be a dearth of such organs, but decisions must not be made by doctors deciding purely on the deserving nature of the recipient. Naturally medical reasons are imperative, but the notion that patients with Down's syndrome – because of their lowered immune system and susceptibility to infection – are more likely to suffer rejection of the organ have been refuted.

The argument that their learning difficulties are likely to pose problems with the compliance of medication or follow up treatment is also flawed in that children have often been the recipients of such organs. A British person with Down's syndrome has yet to undergo this type of surgery and so these doubts about suitability have yet to be tested.

The idea of heart transplants, which seemed so radical not so long ago, now seems almost commonplace and yet still none have been performed in Britain on people with Down's syndrome. The progress that is being made in all aspects of biological science, however, has huge implications for Down's syndrome.

The twenty-first chromosome, which is where the genetic defect of Down's syndrome occurs, is the subject of much interest. Researchers across the world are attempting to 'map out' the full structure of this particular chromosome, identify the specific genes and define their functions.

There are very recent reports that the cognitive difficulties experienced by people with Down's syndrome may be due to an indentifiable gene – the DYRK gene which is necessary for normal brain development in the foetus. At an international scientific conference in Barcelona in March 1997, it was suggested that the gene or genes responsible for many of the physical components of the physical features of Down's syndrome such as congenital heart disease and immunological impairment may be identified.

According to Dr Charles J. Epstein, Chief of Medical Genetics at the University of California:

> There is a reasonable likelihood of developing pharmacological and other forms of therapy that will ameliorate, and perhaps prevent mental retardation [sic] and Alzheimer Disease . . . as we continue to learn more about how the brain works, research on Down's syndrome will be the beneficiary of this knowledge and an understanding of what is impairing the brain in Down's syndrome will eventually be attained . . . research on Down's syndrome in the twenty-first century will be centered in neurobiology, molecular genetics, developmental psychology and molecular pharmacology. We have every reason to be hopeful.

When Sarah was a few months old Allie took her to the Children's Osteopathic Centre in London. Osteopathy is based on holistic principles of maintaining health by balancing procedures which harness the child's individual resources. This can be particularly helpful in ameliorating the immune system, which tends to function less well in children with Down's syndrome. Sarah received some gentle cranial manipulation, designed to open up the airways which are smaller in children with Down's syndrome, who are thus more susceptible to coughs, colds and ear infections. Despite a couple of attacks of croup at a very early age, Sarah has actually rarely had a cold and is generally healthier than her brothers.

Whether cranial osteopathy is the reason for this we shall never know, but *for her* it may have made some difference and this is, I think, the crux of the matter. No matter what the treatment, the main premiss is to remember that, although every person with Down's syndrome is affected by a chromosomal disorder, the effect of having an extra chromosome can cause many individual differences and each person with Down's syndrome should be treated as an individual. No one person with Down's syndrome will have all the ailments associated with the condition. There is no generalized treatment.

As parents, we have a duty to do all in our power for our children. This responsibility becomes an obsession for parents of children with Down's syndrome and other disabilities, who are constantly searching for ways to ameliorate the lives of their children. We must leave no stone unturned and must consider every form of treatment. There may just be a nagging doubt that we are neglecting something that could have a positive effect and to ignore this – no matter how improbable – could be considered unforgivable.

22. My Lucky Man

The web of our life is of a mingled yarn, good and ill together.
(William Shakespeare, *All's Well that Ends Well*)

Sarah treats life like a cocktail party – she mingles and circulates like nobody I know, she possesses her own intoxicating character and like Nicely Nicely is 'known far and wide as a character who dearly loves to commit eating'. When we are in a restaurant or a pub and despite our protestations, Sarah will sometimes approach other children at nearby tables, introduce herself and politely request a roll-call of the other family members.

At the present time her age and charm protect her, but we worry that this over-friendliness could in later years lead to awkward situations. You see, you can't win. We should be rejoicing that she is like this and yet we worry that this is one of the stereotypical traits of behaviour in Down's syndrome and Sarah might be just another victim.

On an occasion, however, when she seemed to be behaving in just this manner, she surprised us again. On her last visit to the Brompton Hospital for a heart scan, we had a two-and-a-half-hour wait to be seen and so we went on a few walkabouts around the hospital. Sarah stopped a number of hospital workers, several of them looking harassed, bored, anxious or distant, and said, 'Hello, what's your name?' Most of their faces lit up and Sarah received her reply and a few more friendly words. We eventually told Sarah to stop bothering these people and that she shouldn't be quite so friendly to strangers. When we finally did see the doctor, he placed the electrodes on her bare chest and whilst playfully tickling her tummy asked, 'Are you ticklish?' Sarah snapped at him, 'Don't!' and he withdrew his hand as if bitten by a piranha.

Sarah has an air of confidence that I envy. She is already her own person and has an independent life separate from us. She loves going to her childminder and school and is disappointed when the weekend arrives and she is stuck with us. She has friends of all ages and quite a few interests. She enjoys dancing, reading and likes singing. (That stereotype about children with Down's syndrome being musical is soon contradicted when you hear Sarah singing her Michael Jackson selection.) She loves playing football, being heavily influenced by her older brother's obsession. During the World Cup qualifying match against Italy, Daniel was singing the words to 'Football's Coming Home'. With her usual mixture of sociability and inquisitiveness, Sarah looked up and said, 'To my house?'

I'm hoping to take her to her first Premiership match soon, although I am slightly worried about how she will react to the crowd, as she is scared of loud noise. When I asked Daniel what he thought, he said, 'Well, if we take her to Spurs we wouldn't have to worry about that.'

Sarah's capacity for warmth and honesty is profound and her enthusiasm is unrivalled. Allie and the children were visiting some friends and Sarah, who adores both their teenage sons, turned to the younger boy whose face is dotted with acne and said admiringly, 'I like your spots.' Despite the personal nature of the remark, surprisingly he seemed to be charmed rather than insulted! Sarah does seem to get away with things that no one else would.

Like any other five-year-old, Sarah can be disobedient and hates to be told off. She is utterly inconsolable when scolded and will cry and cry if she thinks she has done something wrong or if *we* think she has done something wrong. She hates us being cross with her and is desperate to make things better.

Since her dramatic arrival nearly six years ago, Sarah's impact has been extraordinary. She has introduced us to a completely new world where we have met a whole host of new friends and acquaintances – people that we just wouldn't have come across in our 'previous' lives. We have discovered deeper relationships with existing friends and maintained even closer links with our immediate family. My relationship with Allie could not have been tested more by our experiences.

We have learned much about Down's syndrome and disability and have learned even more from the families who cope with the day to day problems of raising a child with a disability. Because of the parents who twenty years ago decided to bring up children with Down's syndrome in their own families, there has been a change in attitude. People with Down's syndrome are achieving more and are much more integrated than ever before. Sarah is reaping the rewards of changing attitudes and gains fought for by previous generations.

The Down's syndrome network is quite remarkable. Apart from the various professional organizations that exist to help parents, subscribing to the Down's syndrome users group on the Internet and reading the mass of encouraging, positive messages is quite humbling. This immediate and worldwide contact must be of great sustenance to new parents who have a thousand questions and can't quite face talking to strangers face to face. I have found myself sharing experiences with a number of fathers with whom I share a common bond and have found myself e-mailing people all over the world.

Following the radio series, we were contacted by a number of parents, who wrote, wanting to share their experiences and I was particularly touched by a letter from a father, whose daughter was only four months old and had found the show helped him in 'articulating the family's thoughts and tapping into a community chest of shared emotions'.

Following an interview in the *Hampstead and Highgate Express*, a local newspaper, my father was contacted by a cousin whom he had not seen for over fifty years. He was reunited with her and other family members. We have since met her and others in the family and I have discovered relatives whom we never knew existed.

By overcoming the pain and fear we felt at her birth we have grown as people. We have been forced to learn patience, understanding and acceptance. We have learned to know people truly as individuals rather than just pay lip service to this notion. The demands have been equalled if not surpassed by the rewards.

Without Sarah none of this would have happened.

When I was a boy aged about ten or eleven, my favourite film was *The Magnificent Seven*, a western starring Yul Brynner and Steve McQueen and based on Kurosawa's film *The Seven Samurai*. Every fortnight, for about a year, my dad would find out where the film was showing and we would set off for unknown parts of London and the Home Counties, ending up in places like Stevenage and Plumstead to pay homage to our heroes. We would take our seats in cold and seedy cinemas and would mouth each scene with affectionate familiarity, knowing exactly what was coming, but always finding something new to admire.

The film is the story of a Mexican farming village regularly terrorized and plundered by a large group of bandits, led by the murderous Calverro (Eli Wallach). The farmers decide to stand up to the bandits and they hire seven gunmen from across the American border to fight Calverro. Although I knew the film backwards (in some of these flea-pits that's exactly how it was shown), there was one scene that I remember in particular and which now seems extremely relevant.

Yul Brynner and Steve McQueen ride out to where the village elder lives. They try to convince the old man that he should take refuge with the rest of the farmers as they are expecting an attack by Calverro and he will be in danger. The old man refuses to leave and says that it is unlikely that the bandits would waste a bullet on him. Asked for his opinion, Steve McQueen's character Vin says that it reminds him of a friend who fell off a ten-storey building and as he was falling, people on each floor heard him say, 'So far so good.'

The simple maxim of 'So far so good' seems right at the moment. I'm not expecting Sarah to carry on falling – but then I don't suppose someone will reach out of an open window and pull her to safety. I have no idea what is going to happen to her.

This is, of course, only half the story and is how I think of her in terms of her emotional, physical and educational progress. It's an experience of worry, uncertainty and hard work. This is the dispassionate view – an intellectual objective assessment and quite different to what I feel about her as my daughter. Then, I run out of superlatives when I think of her calmness, enthusiasm, her laughter and her kind spirit.

Sarah refers to me at the moment as 'My lucky man'. When I've questioned her about what she means, or why I'm so lucky, she's told me that I'm lucky because I can play with her, help her to read, wash her hair, buy her sweets, take her to school and most of all because she likes me! In other words I'm a lucky man because I'm around her. I'm a lucky man because she's my daughter. Somewhat precocious and confident to the point of arrogance, you might think. And yet she's right.

I certainly didn't feel lucky when she was born and I am not one of those people who think that having a child with Down's syndrome was a gift from God. She is not a heaven-sent angel despatched to test my faith and resolve. I do not think that Sarah is the greatest thing that has happened to me. I don't think that she chose Allie and me for her parents – and I'm sure she could have done a lot better than us.

I'm constantly struck by the inconsistencies of experience and ambiguities of feeling in having a child with Down's syndrome. In fact, ambiguity is the name of the game.

Every day I worry about her and wish that we didn't have this extra responsibility. I wish Sarah wasn't going to have to face all these extra problems. I don't want her to find reading and writing such a struggle and yet I'm so proud of her. I wish that she hadn't been born with Down's syndrome, but if she didn't have Down's syndrome she wouldn't be Sarah. I want society to accept her as she is, but I know that in her lifetime, it's more likely that she will have to adapt to society first. I want her to be independent, but I want to protect her. I want her to be treated like everyone else and, unlike Blanche Dubois, I don't want her to have to depend on the kindness of strangers. Conversely, I do also want people to make allowances for her. I want her to be as bright and insightful as possible, but not enough to be aware of how society at large may perceive her. I want to accept Sarah for who she is – with all her faults and limitations – but at the same time I will also do all that I can to extend these boundaries so that she can achieve everything possible.

People say, 'She's really pretty – she can't be badly affected.' Part of me is flattered that my daughter is considered pretty but part of me feels like saying, 'You've missed the point, pal, she has got Down's syndrome and that's part of her and she's beautiful no matter what you think she looks like.' I am aware that the adjustment is incomplete at times and will continue to take on different forms at different stages. Sometimes I am filled with pain for Sarah when I think that she may never experience the kind of life I have had. My deepest wish for her is that she will never feel she has missed out in any way and is happy in the life and love that is her own.

Before conception, no one would choose to have a child with a disability and yet I couldn't possibly choose not to have such a wonderful daughter as Sarah. She is always the first to greet me at the door. 'Nice day at work, Daddy?' (Of course she isn't always quite so concerned if I haven't been working on 'her' book.) If I yawn, she asks me if I'm tired and says, 'Poor Daddy' and if I look sad, she will give me a hug and say, 'Cheer up, Daddy!'

There is one area in which I am completely unequivocal and consistent and biased. My love for her is unambiguous. Sarah, you've been my inspiration in so many ways – least of all you've been my muse. So, if you're reading this and you want to continue to be my goddess of divine influence, now that I've finished the book, I'm looking for work. Oh, no, that's no good, I'm definitely not going to write another book about you. Absolutely not. You see, if there's going to be a sequel in years to come . . .

. . . I want you to write it.

Select Bibliography

Bérubé, Michael, *Life As We Know It*, Pantheon, 1996

Boston, Sarah, *Too Deep for Tears*, Pandora, HarperCollins, 1994

Briggs, Susan, *Those Radio Times*, Weidenfeld and Nicolson, 1981

Burleigh, Michael, *Death and Deliverance, Euthanasia in Germany 1900–1945*, Cambridge University Press, 1994

Burck, C. & Speed, B., *Gender, Power and Relationships*, Routledge, 1995

Cunningham, Cliff, *Down's Syndrome – An Introduction for Parents*, Souvenir Press, 1988

Goodey, C. F. (ed.), *Living in the Real World: Families Speak About Down's Syndrome*, Twenty-one Press, 1991

Kingsley, Jason & Levitz, Mitchell, *Count Us In: Growing Up with Down Syndrome*, Harcourt Brace, 1994

Meyer, Donald J. (ed.), *Uncommon Fathers. Reflections on Raising a Child with a Disability*, Woodbine House, 1995

Moody, Peter & Moody, Roger, *Half Left*, Dreyers Forlag, 1986

Selikowitz, Mark, *Down Syndrome: The Facts*, Oxford University Press, 1990

Stratford, Brian *Down's Syndrome: Past, Present and Future*, Penguin, 1989

Stratford, Brian (ed.), *New Approaches to Down Syndrome*, Cassell, 1996

Trainer, Marilyn, *Differences in Common*, Woodbine House, 1991

Resources

Down's Syndrome Association
155 Mitcham Road
London
SW17 9PG
Tel: 0181-682 4001
Fax: 0181-682 4102
http://www.downs-syndrome.org.uk

Down Syndrome Educational Trust
Sarah Duffen Centre
Belmont Street
Southsea
Portsmouth
Hampshire
PO5 1NA
Tel: 01705-824 261
e-mail: enquiries@downsnet.org
http://www.downsnet.org/

Mencap (Royal Society for Mentally Handicapped Children and Adults)
123 Golden Lane
London
EC1Y 0RT
Tel: 0171-454 0454
Fax: 0171-608 3254

PALACE For All
Scholefield Road
London
N19 3ES
Tel: 0171-561 1689

People First
Instruments House
207–215 King's Cross Road
London
WC1X 9DB
Tel: 0171-713 6400

There are numerous worldwide sites on the Internet, but an excellent place to start is an American parents' and users' list. You can subscribe by sending an e-mail to down-syn@listserv.nodak.edu⁻ and writing: subscribe down-syn <your real name>

UK Down's Syndrome Discussion Forum
To subscribe send an e-mail to:
Ind-downs-syn-uk-list-request@open.ac.uk
In the body of the message type:
subscribe <your e-mail address>